In Search of Runs

In Search of Runs

An Autobiography

Dennis Amiss
with Michael Carey

Stanley Paul, London

Stanley Paul & Co Ltd
3 Fitzroy Square, London W1

An imprint of the Hutchinson Publishing Group

London Melbourne Sydney Auckland
Wellington Johannesburg and agencies
throughout the world

First published 1976
© Dennis Amiss 1976

Set in Monotype Baskerville

Printed in Great Britain by The Anchor Press Ltd
and bound by Wm Brendon & Son Ltd
both of Tiptree, Essex

ISBN 0 09 126780 3

Contents

I

The Formative Years

A privileged start – learning in the league – tearful days in the nets – tuition from 'Tiger' and discipline from Tom – an in-and-out existence – a century and, in 1965, my county cap

Shading my eyes against the glare of the Caribbean sun and brushing away a trickle of perspiration from my cheek, I peered at the ramshackle little scoreboard at Sabina Park, the noisy and colourful cricket ground in Kingston, Jamaica. It confirmed something that I found hard to believe, that England had achieved a cricketing miracle.

We had saved, against all expectations, a Test match against the West Indies. Certain defeat had been turned into a draw with the highest honours and I, Dennis Leslie Amiss, had led the battle for survival for ten hours in making 262 not out.

That was the highest score I had ever made and it was, naturally, the pinnacle of my career as an England batsman, a career which has followed a far from smooth and predictable course. Only eighteen months after that innings, for instance, I was discarded from the England team.

It was not the first time I had sampled failure and despair. And this is not merely a glamorous story of soaring success and unlimited runs. Nor is it a cricketing tale of rags to riches.

Like any other man who plays a demanding game for a living, I have known both the heights and the depths. As a professional in a sport that has become tougher and more competitive than ever, even in my time, I have proved no less vulnerable to the quirks of fate and fortune than any other human being.

In telling this story, I have tried to be truthful and objective. I have not raked around for dressing-room gossip or behind-the-scenes scandal, but where I have been in a position to offer a personal, pertinent view of something or someone of interest I have tried to do so.

My career with Warwickshire and England has, for example, encompassed a revolutionary era in county cricket. It has changed so drastically that now we play in not one competition, but four. On a wider front, the world's cricketing nations have taken part in a one-day international tournament that must have been undreamed of years ago.

In my time, too, I have played with and against some players who are probably among the greatest the game has ever known. Names like Sir Garfield Sobers and Barry Richards spring to mind. I have tasted the drama and excitement of Test Cricket in many parts of the world.

More recently, I have been face to face with two of the fastest bowlers ever to play in the same team, Dennis Lillee and Jeff Thomson. And opening the innings with Geoff Boycott has, perhaps, given me more insight than many people into what makes him one of the game's most enigmatic characters.

These are some aspects of modern English cricket that I have been privileged to experience. In using that privilege to tell this story I have endeavoured to be fair to my fellow cricketers, of all countries, and above all to be honest with myself.

When this book appears I will be embarking upon a cricket season which could well decide whether I have a future as an England player. It is not the first time my Test career has been clouded with doubt and uncertainty, but at least I have had a Test career and for that I shall always be grateful.

There have been times, as you will read, when I despaired of ever making runs for Warwickshire or England. There were also moments when I made them by the hundred. I have tried to be philosophical about success and failure and at all times I have never forgotten those who have helped me on my way.

In the early days – the formative years, if you like – my father Victor gave me every encouragement. He was a good club cricketer who played for Birmingham Co-op on Saturdays and on Sundays for Harps, an itinerant team with no ground of their own for whom Butch White, later to join Hampshire as a fast bowler, batted at number three.

So I grew up in a cricketing environment and with more privileges and opportunities than many boys of my age. My father, who worked in the family tyre business, was enthusiastic enough to buy all my equipment and, as a member of Warwickshire, to pay for my coaching at Edgbaston at the age of nine.

By the time I was fifteen, having been coached by 'Tiger' Smith and Derief Taylor and having enjoyed some success in schools cricket, I was offered a contract to join the Warwickshire junior staff. In many households the thought of a son wanting to take up such a hazardous, modestly paid profession as county cricket would not have gone down at all well.

Ours was different. Everybody was all in favour. It was just as well because I had always wanted to become a professional cricketer and no other career appealed to me. I was fortunate, too, that there was the family tyre business to fall back on and to provide me with a job out of season.

The summer of 1958, therefore, found me on the Warwickshire nursery staff, selling scorecards at Test matches and chasing famous players (many of whom I have since played against) for their autographs. I played in the Club and Ground side – in those days I was also classed as a bowler – and for Smethwick in the Birmingham League.

Cyril Goodway, now the Warwickshire chairman, was the Smethwick captain and he thought league cricket was a good background for a young player. They play it hard and you also come across many high-class players from whom you can learn. In my case they included Eric Hollies, Roly Jenkins, Basil D'Oliveira and Tom Graveney.

Gradually I moved up to the Warwickshire second team where I found the game extremely hard because of the better class of bowling. It was a struggle to make runs, but eventually I held my place, helped by the priceless assistance that 'Tiger' Smith and Tom Dollery, the head coach and second-team captain, were always ready to provide.

'Tiger', for instance, was marvellous when it came to analysing a batsman's technique. At that time I could not play very effectively on the leg side and more than once 'Tiger', whose manner was brusque but sincere, reduced me to tears as he bellowed instructions at me in the nets.

One day, to prove his point, he asked Roly Thompson and Jack Bannister, two of the Warwickshire fast bowlers, to let a few go at his legs as quickly as they could . . . even though, at the age of sixty, he was not wearing pads. Eventually they cracked him on the knee and left him hopping about. 'Never mind about missing the ball,' he said. 'That's the way to play.'

I took his words to heart and, just as importantly, 'Tiger' never over-coached me. With me, as with any young player, he always tried to bring out whatever natural ability there was, while Tom Dollery, with his wartime experiences in the Army never far away from his thoughts, was the ideal disciplinarian to control the young tearaways under his charge in the second team.

After a hard day in the field, for instance, he would silence our complaints by recalling the time he travelled 120 miles by jeep across a desert with a ration of one cup of water, to be used for shaving, topping up the radiator and – if there was any left – refreshment.

Once, after a slight case of disorderly behaviour in our hotel during the evening of an away match, he made us line up outside in twos the following morning and quick-marched us to the ground three miles away. We soon got the message.

Most of the time, Tom's discipline was tempered by his great sense of humour. As you probably know, my running between the wickets has not always been flawless and one day, during a Club and Ground match in the Birmingham area, Tom took me to one side and led me into the pavilion.

He pointed to a framed scorecard on the wall. In one innings was the line: A. V. Amiss run out 0. Tom looked at me and said: 'I'll never blame you for another run out, Dennis – it's hereditary!'

On another occasion, when rain interrupted a second team match at Peterborough, some of us passed the time on a nearby bowling green. Tom noticed this and with just the right amount of sarcasm in his voice he shouted to me: 'Amiss, I wish you would master one game before trying to play another!'

Tom was also an excellent captain, shrewd with his field placings and tactically always appearing to be one move ahead of the opposition. Under his leadership I developed and in 1960 began playing well enough to be picked for my first championship match, against Surrey at the Oval.

That game will be in the record books for a long time, not on my account but because Norman Horner and Billy Ibadulla together put on a record first-wicket partnership of 377, every run of which was watched by a nervous Amiss who, being then classed as an all-rounder, was down to bat at number six.

I never actually got to the wicket, but had my first bowl, dismissing Eric Bedser. As we were in the field for two days, my first impressions of county cricket were not too favourable. Nor did I enjoy the next match when I was run out for nought without facing a ball.

In the next few seasons, with so many good batsmen on the Warwickshire staff, I was in and out of the first team. I slipped a disc and was forced to give up bowling (I still feel it if I try to bowl today) and in 1964, with my career apparently at a standstill, I seriously considered calling it a day.

I was still struggling to make runs, could no longer be seriously thought of as a bowler and there seemed no way I could get into the strong Warwickshire team as a batsman alone. It began to look like the family tyre business after all.

But before the start of the 1965 season both Ray Hitchcock and Norman Horner retired and I decided it was worth persevering. At the start of the summer I was given six matches in the first team, which, importantly for a young player, enabled me to go out and bat without being too concerned about the consequences of failure.

Batting first wicket down, I made seventy-odd against Glamorgan on a wet wicket and followed this with a century against Oxford University. Other reasonable performances followed and later that season I was awarded my county cap.

I was so thrilled that for several nights I went to bed wearing it, along with my Warwickshire sweater for good measure. I prized them so highly that I was not going to risk anyone taking them from me!

By the end of that season I had completed a thousand runs for the first time. In those days I simply went out and batted without giving much thought to the technique and methods I was employing.

I must have thought then that county cricket was such a carefree, uncomplicated way of life. Little did I dream of the struggles and nightmares that lay ahead.

2

An England Batsman . . . or am I?

Surprise choice for England in 1966 series v. West Indies – high praise from Sobers – the turmoil of a Test début – a night out with Graveney – my first tour and a record season – big-match nerves and failures – that 'pair' at Old Trafford – encouragement from Cowdrey and Insole

Naturally, I had always hoped to play for England one day, but even though I began the 1966 season by scoring my fair share of runs, it never occurred to me to think of myself as an England player. For one thing, this was only my second full season and Test selectors – especially English Test selectors – rarely take a chance on comparative newcomers.

Another factor (although I did not appreciate it at the time) was that I was making plenty of sixties and seventies and was quite content with them. I was happy to go on playing my shots and not particularly displeased when I kept getting out short of three figures.

That was a flaw in my make-up, but I did not realize it at the time. I soon learned that to develop the art of batsmanship you needed to be able to play a long innings. It gives you confidence and, young players may care to note, the longer you bat the more likely you are to produce strokes you never thought you possessed.

So to say I was surprised when I was named for the final Test against the West Indies is putting it mildly. As we were three down in the series, the selectors were under some pressure, but even so when John Moxley, a Birmingham journalist, rang me up to congratulate me on my selection I asked him as politely as possible to stop joking.

Coincidentally, Warwickshire were in the middle of a game against the West Indies that week-end. I had made only nineteen the previous day, which had done nothing to make me think my name was in the minds of the selectors, and it was only when I saw the morning paper the next day that the news began to sink in.

Curiously enough, this method of hearing whether you are in or out of a Test team or touring party still applies today. Many people must think we receive embossed invitations from Lord's or, at very least, telegrams or phone calls, but the fact is we do not.

Some years ago the selectors used to sound out players by writing to ask if they were available for a tour. You knew then that you were on the short list. Now you just have to sweat it out with the rest of the cricketing public, though afterwards you do receive a letter of confirmation.

In my case, I switch on the radio or television and keep my fingers crossed. Since the names are given in alphabetical order, the agony is soon over for me once they have named the captain and vice-captain.

The reason players are not notified in advance, I believe, is to prevent 'leaks' to the Press, which have happened in the past. Even when Alan Smith, my own county captain, was a Test selector he would never breathe a word to me about my selection.

Most players are too thrilled to be chosen to worry about the formalities, anyway. The news certainly had an effect on me. In the second innings of that West Indies game, moving up from number three to open for the first time, I made 160 not out.

A remark made by Gary Sobers and passed on by a colleague also encouraged me. He thought I was the most promising young English player he had seen and thought I should be in the Test team. You rarely get to know what other people – not to mention the world's greatest all-rounder – think of your ability.

So I drove down to the Oval in a state of high excitement and growing nervousness. My mind was in a whirl. I could hardly wait to set eyes on my England tie and sweaters. I wondered which famous player would be sharing a room with me.

It turned out to be Ken Higgs, who was the only man to play in every Test in that series. His first words when I met him at our hotel were: 'Congratulations – I'll take the big bed and you can have the small one!'

That night I found myself listening, overawed, to players like Boycott, Graveney and D'Oliveira discussing the game at the usual eve-of-Test dinner. Not surprisingly, little or nothing was heard from D. L. Amiss; after all, only a few years earlier he had been collecting the autographs of some of his new team-mates.

Nor did I get much sleep that night. While Higgs snored blissfully, my mind turned over the endless questions which no doubt occur to every player on the night before his first appearance for England: would I get off the mark or – horror of horrors – out first ball?

Would Sobers get me out with his big inswinger and would Wes Hall come hurtling in to bowl really fast? Where would I field? Supposing I dropped a catch off someone who went on to make a century? Would I even get my pads on in time to bat? What if I were to cost England the match by not getting out to the middle quickly enough!

As you will gather, my brain was in a turmoil. Some of the thoughts may seem trivial, but any amount of players *do* forget the little things. Batsmen frequently reach the middle before realizing they are not wearing a protector. Not long ago, a Worcestershire player walked out without his bat.

The next morning, having hardly slept at all, I was up early, had a net and returned to the dressing-room for a change of clothes and a cup of coffee. This has remained my routine on the morning of any match; indeed, I believe in having as much net practice as possible.

Opinions vary on this. Some players feel they can get by without practice when they are in action seven days a week. But Sir Donald Bradman, Herbert Sutcliffe and Tom Graveney were three who believed in regular practice and their philosophy will do for me. Any young batsman who doubts it should try learning to play the piano or violin without practice and see how far he gets.

We lost the toss, so my first Test innings had to wait. I doubt that I was too worried about that! When it eventually arrived I walked past Wes Hall on the way out and heard him say: 'Good luck, young man.' Later, I was leg-before to him for seventeen.

Under the circumstances I could hardly have expected to

do better. I was – and I am not ashamed to admit it – completely overawed by the occasion and by the company I was keeping. But as England won by an innings and thirty-four runs I tried not to let my own modest contribution worry me too much.

My one outstanding memory of that Test concerns Tom Graveney. He had played handsomely to make 165, and that evening, spotting me uneasily having a drink in the committee room (I still felt very much out of things), he suggested I join Ken Higgs, Basil D'Oliveira and himself for dinner.

I was thrilled at the thought. This was my first night out as an England player and I had been invited to dine with the great Tom Graveney. No doubt he would be wanting to celebrate his marvellous innings with a bottle or two of wine, perhaps even champagne.

Visions of a sumptuous feast in an elegant restaurant, accompanied by revealing cricket anecdotes, swept over me. Graveney drove the four of us along the Edgware Road heading, I thought, back to our hotel restaurant which seemed opulent enough for the occasion.

Suddenly he pulled to the kerb. 'Here we are,' said Graveney, leaping out. We were outside a fish-and-chip shop. 'This is a great place,' Tom went on. 'Pie and chips, bread and butter and a cup of tea, all for five bob! Where can you get better value than that?'

That winter I went on the England under-25 tour to Pakistan feeling that by making the breakthrough to the Test team I had taken a step in the right direction. This tour provided valuable experience, not only at cricket but also of the pleasures and pitfalls of touring, and I would like to see them take place more often for the benefit of up-and-coming players.

Most of us suffered from stomach trouble sooner or later, though Keith Fletcher was an exception. He seems to have a cast-iron constitution which no country in the world can disturb. It was also, as you might expect, fiercely hot all the time, which seemed to surprise Richard Hutton who carried with him everywhere a camel-hair overcoat, as if expecting rain or snow.

That wasn't Hutton's only odd experience. One night we arrived at our hotel late after a long trip and he wasted no time in going to bed after first instructing the man on the reception desk that he and his room-mate would like tea for two at ten o'clock the next morning.

You can imagine his consternation when he was awakened by a fearful hammering on his door in the middle of the night. He opened it and was greeted by a grinning Pakistani carrying a huge tray which threatened to collapse under the weight of a vast amount of crockery and teapots.

As Hutton glared at him he said politely: 'Here you are, sir – tea for ten at two, as requested!'

Back home in 1967, I made 1850 runs batting first wicket down for Warwickshire. This remains my best aggregate for a season – with less championship cricket I doubt if I will surpass it – but I was picked for the second Test against India only because Geoff Boycott had been dropped for slow scoring in making his 246.

Ken Barrington moved up to replace him and, batting in the middle order, I played in two Tests against India and one against Pakistan. Time after time I brought about my own downfall with one bad stroke after another and I was twelfth man in the other Tests, obviously to give me a gradual acclimatization to the England scene.

But I was still horribly nervous. Significantly, in the last Test against Pakistan I detected a slight improvement, and this was, I think, because Barrington had taken the trouble to walk down the pitch to give me some advice and to try to calm me down.

This was the first time any other England player had tried to help me. Ironically I was dropped twice in the second innings, though I scored only three not out. England needed only fourteen to win and it was an awkward situation for a young player trying to establish himself in the team. I had precious little to gain and everything to lose, yet I had to bat because Graveney did not want to.

All the self-doubt came back again after that. It was, as I have said, my best-ever season, but I still could not make runs for England. The constant theme was that I did not possess the right temperament to do it at Test level; I felt that one decent score was all that I needed to break through.

I was quite sure that nerves were at the heart of my struggle. When people began dissecting my temperament I probably began trying too hard, too. Analysing my dismissals, which included once chopping the ball on to my foot and then on to the wicket, I also felt I had hardly enjoyed beginner's luck.

While I was all too aware that there was a long way to go, I still felt there was nothing much wrong that one long innings for England could not put right. And Brian Close, the England captain, had told me privately that if he were asked to take the MCC party to the West Indies that winter he would want me in it.

Ironically, Close lost the captaincy after an incident in a game at Edgbaston in which I was playing, and when the tour party was named I was not among them. It knocked the wind out of my sails, and it was probably then that I began to realize that there was much more to the business of playing Test cricket than I had appreciated.

At the same time I was conscious of having always been on trial, always playing for my place. It would have helped – and this still applies to young players today – if I had been told I was to play for a couple of Tests, regardless of how I fared.

At that stage a tour would have done me immense good. Away from home you have the feeling of belonging to the tour party and you know you are bound to play now and again. Equally importantly, I think, you do not feel the eyes of the English public are scrutinizing your every move, waiting for you to make a mistake.

After spending part of that winter touring East Africa with a team raised by Joe Lister, then secretary of Worcestershire, I did not have an outstanding season in 1968. Early on, however, I was playing well enough to be picked for the first Test against Australia at Old Trafford . . . a game I will never forget.

It brought me something that every batsman dreads – a 'pair'. What is more, this was the first time it had happened to me in any class of cricket and now I had bagged 'em against Australia – in front of some highly cynical spectators, too.

I can hear now the scornful remarks made by some of the Lancashire members – loud enough to make sure I knew about them – as I completed that long walk back to the pavilion after the second nought. 'He can't play' and 'He should never be an England player' were just two of them.

How did it happen? In the first innings I was batting with Colin Cowdrey, who came down the pitch to advise me how to combat Graham McKenzie who was bowling pretty quickly

B

and moving the ball about. Cowdrey suggested I should follow his example and move back and across to cover the off stump.

I was grateful for the advice but thought I would be better sticking to my own method of not committing myself until I had picked up the length and line of the ball. Then I played a pathetic stroke outside the off stump without moving my feet and was caught at slip.

In the second innings Bob Cowper was turning his off-breaks slightly and the Australians crowded me, sensing – rightly – that I was very anxious to get off the mark. Seeing a gap on the legside I tried to play a pick-up off my toes but chose the wrong ball – a yorker – and was bowled.

Back in the dressing-room I was near to tears despite the efforts of the rest of the team to reassure me. 'You're a player now that you've bagged 'em,' someone said heartily. I did not agree. I thought my Test career was over.

Obviously I was not picked again for that series. I returned to Warwickshire, did not play particularly well and started to think more and more about my batting technique. Yet I still knew that my frame of mind, my anxiety, had contributed to the bad strokes I had played at Old Trafford.

I also went back to the last cricketer who had reduced me to tears – 'Tiger' Smith. He tried to restore my self-confidence and he also pointed out that I was not watching the ball from the bowler's hand but off the pitch as if I was expecting every delivery to 'explode' at me.

That, of course, is a typical symptom of the out-of-form batsman. For the rest of that season I struggled so much that I did not bother to listen to the radio for the names of the MCC party to tour Pakistan. I knew mine would not be among them.

Ah well, I thought, I shall have to settle for being just another county cricketer now. But there was a slight ray of hope. In my mail at the end of the season were letters from Doug Insole, the chairman of selectors, and Colin Cowdrey, who had regained the England captaincy and was to lead the party in Pakistan.

Both wrote that they thought, despite my failures, that I was still good enough to come back one day and make runs at Test level. As I settled down to a winter of selling tyres, it was heartening to think that at least two influential personalities in the world of cricket still had faith in my ability.

3

My Debt to the Indians

Why I captained Warwickshire in 1969 – Knott teaches me a lesson – my attitude to 'walking' – dropped by Warwickshire and I almost retire – I move up to open and win a tour place – the make-believe match that changed my life – two centuries and an armed guard in the 1973 series in Pakistan

Knowing that Colin Cowdrey and Doug Insole were confident that I had a future as a Test batsman was one thing. Developing that confidence in my own ability was another, and throughout the next season – 1969 – I was still experimenting with my technique, trying as it were to discover the real Amiss.

Not surprisingly, I had only a moderate season, making just over a thousand runs at an average of around thirty. This might have seemed satisfactory to some players, but not to me; at the back of my mind I felt it was going to be difficult to become a consistent county batsman, let alone established in the England team.

In view of that, plus my comparative lack of experience, I was rather startled one day when Alan Smith, the Warwickshire captain, called me into his office and said he would like me to skipper the side when his duties as a Test selector took him away.

It turned out that I was not exactly first choice. Jack Bannister was, in fact, the official club vice-captain at the time but he was not a regular member of the team then, partly because of injury and partly because of the presence of David Brown, Norman McVicker and Bill Blenkiron.

Tom Cartwright, who was next in seniority, had turned the

job down. So had Jim Stewart. Billy Ibadulla and John Jameson, who were both senior to me, were not even approached.

I agreed to lead the side provided I could be sure of 100 per cent support from those players who had declined the position. So I became captain of Warwickshire for six matches. We won two and were denied by the weather in two more, but I will not pretend that I took to the job like a born leader.

When we were on top and I was able to set aggressive fields I found the job relatively easy. But I was not so good at deciding when we should close the game up and go on the defensive, and this only confirmed my theory that good captains take years to master the art.

In my case I had also to handle a team which included one or two really hard-headed old-time professionals. When we were doing well life was great. When things went wrong they tended to say: 'Well, skipper, you're in charge – you get us out of this mess!'

So I was not too sorry when the time came to hand back to A. C. Smith, though like every cricketer I had a few ideas of my own and took the chance to try them out. Once, for instance, I persuaded Billy Ibadulla, who normally bowled medium pace or off-spinners, to experiment with leg-breaks which he had been practising in the nets.

We were playing Sussex on a typically placid Edgbaston pitch. Billy came on, managed to drop the ball in the rough outside the off stump and dismissed two left-handers, Mike Buss and Ken Suttle. We went on to win the match.

Before I had time to consider myself a rising tactical genius, however, I was brought down to earth when we lost our next match – against Scotland! We fielded virtually a second team, but that did not stop Tom Dollery exploding. 'Oh, no,' he said. 'You can't lose to Scotland. What a disgrace!'

Meanwhile I pressed on with my uneven career as a batsman. The following year Mike Smith came out of retirement and I found myself batting at number five. Though I scored some 1300 runs I was not happy with this arrangement.

I thought that number four should have been my place and not Mike's, simply because he was an accomplished player with most of his career behind him while I was still learning. With many teams of course, number five would have been ideal, but Warwickshire's strong batting meant that often I did not have time to play a proper innings.

In 1971, though, I found myself back on the Test scene. It was still a struggle, even though the selectors considerately told me I would play in the first two matches against Pakistan regardless of how many – or how few – runs I scored.

In three innings I made only four, twenty-two and nineteen and then, at last, in the third Test at Headingley, came my first half-century for England. Oddly enough, even that milestone could not entirely wipe out the feeling that the occasion was too much for me, that I was still overawed and it was not the real me who was walking out to bat.

Then, in the first Test against India who were the second visitors that year, I learned from Alan Knott a salutary lesson about batting in international cricket. He and I were batting together when I was caught behind for not very many off Bishen Bedi.

As I played at the ball I also caught my boot with my bat. There was such a loud, confident appeal that I was convinced that I must have got an edge and 'walked' immediately. But back in the dressing-room Knott tore a huge strip off me.

'What the — hell do you think you are doing walking when you didn't hit the ball?' he stormed. 'Don't forget, this is a *Test* match.'

He then explained that I had missed the ball by some distance and should have waited for the umpire's decision. That episode made me think about 'walking', a controversial subject in recent years, and one which can only be an essentially personal issue between a batsman and his conscience.

I have always believed in walking, in any class of cricket, provided I am absolutely certain that I have hit the ball. Since that day I have walked – even in Test cricket – but if there has been the slightest suggestion of doubt I have been happy to let the umpire decide.

Keith Boyce, of Essex and the West Indies, may smile to himself when he reads that because even now he believes he had me caught behind off a short-pitched ball when I made 262 not out in Jamaica, an innings which I will discuss in greater detail later.

The point about that episode was that I felt that the ball *might* have brushed my gloves, but I could not be certain amid all the clamour and tension of the occasion. With not only a Test match but an entire series at stake I would have been a fool to walk – and the umpire gave me not out.

But Keith Boyce has never forgotten. Though we are good friends off the field, he still lets me have a generous ration of bouncers when we are in opposition as a reminder of the day when he was convinced he should have had my wicket in a Test match.

When I failed to score in the second innings of that Leeds Test I sensed that the axe would fall again, and so it did. That was the end of Test cricket for me that year and when the Australians arrived in 1972 I never expected to be considered for an England place.

What I did not bargain for, however, was losing my place in the Warwickshire team, even though there was more competition because Alvin Kallicharran, who was already being spoken of as a high-class player, had qualified and John Whitehouse had emerged as a talented young batsman the previous year.

I had hardly helped my own cause by batting moderately in the first two matches of the season, against the Universities, but even so I felt the decision to leave me out had been taken rather hastily. I felt very bitter about it.

So began another low point in my career. I decided that there was nothing to be gained from allowing a chip to develop on my shoulder and realized that the quickest way – indeed the only way – back to the first team would be on the strength of as many runs as possible in the second eleven.

I was wrong. Though I made several centuries, I was still not recalled, even though there were some first-team players who were obviously out of touch. Once again I found myself in Alan Smith's office, this time to discuss my future.

When he told me there was nothing he could do because other players had to be given a reasonable run in the first team, there seemed little point in staying with Warwickshire. I did not want to leave them, but if I could not get into the first team when I was playing well a move to another county or giving up completely seemed the only options left to me.

This probably sounds like the typically selfish attitude of a self-centred young sportsman, but I was concerned about the future. I had a wife and daughter to consider. I certainly could not provide for my family on the wages I was earning as a second-team player.

I also felt that after more than ten years at Edgbaston I had played quite enough second-team cricket and was in some danger of becoming stale. If I was going to develop it would only be in the first team where the level of skill and competitiveness was greater.

Eventually it occurred to me that my one chance was to volunteer to open the innings. I had never considered myself as an opening batsman – not even when I made that century for Warwickshire against the West Indies – but at this stage neither John Whitehouse nor John Jameson was making runs consistently.

When I put the idea to Alan Smith he agreed. To complete a sudden and happy change of fortunes, in my first innings as a regular opener I made 151 not out against Middlesex, though I enjoyed a lot of luck. That innings was yet another illustration of the thin line between failure and success.

If I had been dismissed early on, when I was regularly playing and missing, my career might have ended there and then. But I settled in on a good pitch and all my missing self-confidence came flooding back, especially when I made 192 against Lancashire, which was then the highest score of my career.

The season ended on an even happier note when I was picked to play in the first Prudential Trophy one-day game against Australia at Old Trafford. I was as surprised and delighted by this piece of news as I had been dismayed about being left out by Warwickshire.

I could only put it down to the fact that I had a reasonable record in one-day cricket. Even so, I felt sorry for Barry Wood who had just made ninety in the fifth Test. After all, this was his home ground – and everyone knew what I had achieved on my last appearance against Australia there!

I walked out to bat feeling reassured that at least I could do no worse than my 'pair' in 1968 – not in a one-day match! In fact, I made a century which was widely praised, though I knew I was lucky early on that I did not see too much of Dennis Lillee and was within an inch or so of being 'gloved' by Bob Massie.

Suddenly I was an England cricketer again. My successful

come-back, although in one-day internationals, earned me a place in the MCC party that went to India and Pakistan that winter. This was my first full tour and one which was to have plenty of colour, excitement and controversy, but for me the pattern became disturbingly familiar – after three Test matches I lost my place again.

This time it was not so much due to a shortage of self-confidence as to a lack of experience against high-class spin bowling on unfamiliar Indian pitches. Having made my fair share of runs in England the previous summer, I now found myself baffled by an entirely different game of cricket.

The Indian spinners would come on after only two overs of the new ball. They crowded fielders round the bat and with some balls turning and some not – one of the most difficult types of pitch to bat on – it was small wonder that Barry Wood and myself struggled.

Two batsmen whose experience might have showed us the way, Geoff Boycott and John Edrich, had declined to go on tour, so we had to work things out for ourselves. By the time we reached Kanpur my confidence had ebbed away again and I was left out of the Test team, but this – though I did not realize it at the time – was to lead to yet another turning point in my career.

Hour after hour batting in the nets, without the prospect of getting to the middle, merely made me stale. Jack Birkenshaw also spent day after day in the nets, cheerfully willing to bowl at anyone at any time. One day we arrived at a fresh hotel to find each bed equipped with a mosquito net. This was too much for Jack. 'Not only do I spend all day bowling in 'em,' he said. 'Now I have to sleep in the bloody things as well!'

Though we lost that series it was a fine tour in every other aspect. Hospitality was high-class and many friendships were formed. In my case, this had a special significance.

When we reached Bombay, I found myself discussing my batting failures with some of the Indian players. Three of them, Abid Ali, Bishen Bedi and Venkataraghavan, said it might help if they were to bowl at me and after the Test was over, there being no other nets available, they set one up in the middle of the Brabourne Stadium.

The pitch at Bombay had been the worst of the series and the one in the net was useful to bowl on, too. For the next hour

A surprise choice for England. Garry (now Sir Garfield) Sobers congratulates me on being selected for my first Test, against the West Indies, in 1966.

Champion days. Three members of the only championship winning
Warwickshire teams reminisce at the celebrations for our 1972 win. With me
are 'Tiger' Smith, who played in the 1911 side, and Tom Pritchard, a member of
the 1951 team.

Three Warwickshire smiles. John Jameson, Bob Willis and myself after hearing
news of our selection to tour the West Indies in 1974. Our fortunes were to be
mixed.

Meeting Her Majesty. I am introduced to the Queen by England captain
Ray Illingworth during the Lord's Test against India in 1971.

In Adelaide during the 1974–75 tour Sir Donald Bradman presents me with
the Lord's Taverners tie after being voted their cricketer of the year for 1974.
Alec Bedser, MCC manager, looks on.

Above left: John Snow, fast bowler and poet. How pleased the West Indians were when we left him out of our Test team. *Above right:* Ray Illingworth. The best captain I have played under. *Below left:* Sir Garfield Sobers. The greatest all-rounder ever, but his presence meant more to the West Indies than just runs and wickets. *Below right:* The unlikely-looking Test hero. David Steele hooks Lillee for four at Lord's in the 1975 Test against Australia.

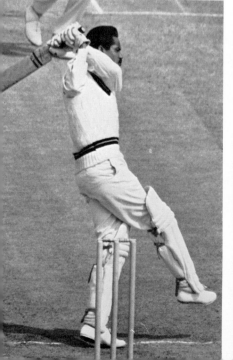

or so, the three Indian bowlers and myself played a make-believe Test match in the middle of that deserted ground.

I suppose we must have seemed like a bunch of schoolboys, imagining themselves as famous Test players. But it was a deadly serious affair because I had asked the Indians to put everything into their bowling, as if they were trying to get me out in a Test match.

We pretended that they had close fielders around the bat and, at my suggestion, they appealed for everything that could have got me out. It was a remarkable – and I suppose some people might think, crazy – episode but today I am in no doubt about the way it influenced my technique and my attitude towards Test cricket.

Such a lengthy, concentrated session against three high-class bowlers enabled me to adjust my methods, especially against the turning ball. More than anything, I think, it taught me to play every ball on its merits. The only unfortunate aspect was that some of those bowlers have since suffered at my hands for their generosity and kindness.

I was soon able to put my newly acquired methods and knowledge into practice when we moved on to Pakistan, where I at last made my first century in Test cricket. This naturally gave me much pleasure but my enjoyment of the occasion was tempered by the fact that threats had been made on the safety of the MCC party.

Before we left India, Donald Carr, our manager, received a telegram which read: 'Do not let Amiss play in Pakistan. B.S.' We took the initials to stand for Black September, the international terrorist organization, though why they had singled out a batsman who had made no impact on the series in India still baffles me.

But the result was that the MCC party was provided with an armed escort both in India and in Pakistan – and because I was named in the telegram I became probably the first English cricketer ever to have his own personal bodyguard.

I was introduced to him on our arrival in Pakistan and afterwards became accustomed to being shadowed everywhere. In the morning I would poke my head out of the bedroom door and he would be there, his gun at the ready.

At night, in the hotel dining-room, he would sit unobtrusively at an adjacent table. He travelled to and from the various cricket grounds with me and when I went out to bat I half expected to find him there, too.

Like most people in that part of the world, he was a fanatic about cricket and we inevitably became good friends. Happily he was not called upon to use his gun on my behalf, and at the end of the tour I gave him signed photographs of myself and the rest of the MCC players for his wife and family.

By then I at last felt I was on my way as an England player. I had played well in Sri Lanka between the two series and in the first Test against Pakistan at Lahore I was relieved to find a better pitch with the quicker bowlers having a greater share of the action – in short, a more familiar game to an Englishman on his first tour.

This was just as well because, like many members of the party, I was not exactly in the best of health. In fact, after a bout of what is euphemistically referred to as stomach trouble, I was confined to bed with a temperature less than twenty-four hours before the Test started.

But I recovered enough to play and was in luck when I was dropped in the slips at fifty. Putting this out of my mind, I moved through the sixties and seventies, and, sensing my first Test hundred ahead, settled down to make sure I reached it. Happily, I managed it without going into my shell, which would have been to the detriment of the team's performance.

My one uneasy moment was self-inflicted. I suddenly remembered that on the earlier, under-25 tour of Pakistan I had recovered from dysentery to play, only to be caught off a full toss at ninety-nine. I made sure *that* did not happen this time.

Next came Hyderabad and the hottest weather I have ever experienced anywhere in the world during a cricket match. The temperature rose to 120 degrees in the shade; it was like batting in a furnace as the heat reared up into your face, stinging the eyes, from a parched, grassless pitch.

We survived, somehow, on what seemed to be an endless diet of drinks and salt tablets, and my contribution to an England total of 487 was 158. This was gratifying, but in that heat and after my illness this innings left me so exhausted that I was ordered to bed for the next two days, while my team-mates sweltered as Pakistan replied with 569.

The first two Tests were drawn. So was the third at Karachi, but under different circumstances. Because of rioting, 100 minutes were lost and a dust-storm caused its early abandonment, but it was unique in that Mushtaq Mohammad, Majid Khan and myself each made ninety-nine.

Three centuries in successive Test matches would have been wonderful compensation for all my early failures, but missing the third – even by a solitary run – was only a minor disappointment. For the first time in my mercurial England career, I began to feel at home.

But I was far from complacent. I knew that even greater challenges now lay ahead and because I had at last proved my right to an England place, consistent top-class performances would be demanded of me in the future.

4

Who Captains England?

*Playing for England creates new problems – the battle between Illing-
worth and Lewis in the 1973 Test trial – why I would have picked
Boycott – New Zealand almost make history – humiliated by the
West Indies – the best captain I have played under – and the one who
had the roughest ride ever*

More than at any other time in my career I relished the
prospect of the next English summer, with the visits of New
Zealand and the West Indies, but by playing in every Test
Match for the first time I experienced a problem I had never
encountered before.

Because of Test matches, I appeared in only ten county
championship matches for Warwickshire, scoring just under
500 runs at an average of forty-one. I did not hit even one
century for them and, overall, it was not the sort of contribution
you might expect from a current England batsman.

But there was an explanation, if not an excuse. I found it
difficult to adjust from playing cricket at Test level, with its
heightened pressures and tensions, to the less-demanding
tempo of the county game, especially in a team that was not in
the running for honours.

Of course, I wanted to do well for Warwickshire, but that
summer I felt as though I was playing two different types of
cricket for two different clubs, rather as a club cricketer
notices the difference between league cricket on Saturdays
and friendlies on Sundays. Each time I returned to Edgbaston
there was probably, too, a tendency to unwind, a subconscious
relaxing of concentration after the Test match.

This is something you have to learn to live with. In later years I think I managed to do it, but I believe this is a factor which can affect the performances of many players, especially younger ones, in an era when we play so much Test and international cricket while the county championship has been allowed to dwindle.

The 1973 season began with a Test trial at Hove between England (picked from players who had been on tour) and The Rest. I made a century before giving my wicket away – not without some misgivings – on the instructions of Alec Bedser, the chairman of selectors, but the most intriguing aspect of this match concerned the respective claims for the England captaincy of Tony Lewis and Ray Illingworth.

Lewis, who had led the MCC party to India and Pakistan and had not done at all badly with a below-strength team, captained England in the trial. Illingworth, who had missed the tour because of business reasons, led The Rest – but for the first Test against New Zealand he was named as captain, with Lewis picked to play under him.

I felt that Lewis was unlucky to lose the captaincy so abruptly but, examining the situation logically, it made sense to me that if we were picking the best available captain, then Illingworth had to be reinstated.

I have never wanted to opt out of an MCC tour and I assumed that Illingworth – and Boycott and Edrich for that matter – had good reasons which were acceptable to the selectors. My view is that these factors should not influence the thinking of the selectors and the best available team should always be chosen.

On the other hand, I would not want to encourage players to become *prima donnas*, continually picking and choosing where and when *they* want to play. It is a subject which demands common sense and clear thinking and yet it is not one for which you can draw up a set of hard-and-fast rules.

For instance, in 1975, knowing what we would be up against from the Australians, I would not have hesitated to pick Geoff Boycott if he had declared himself available – despite his withdrawal from the previous winter's tour. But I know there were some who would not have considered him at any price.

At Trent Bridge in 1973 I felt sorry for Lewis, who after

doing reasonably well as a batsman on the tour now found himself having to play for his place. No wonder he was nervous and subdued, in contrast to his normal character, throughout that match. He did not play as well as he could, dropped a catch and, usually fielding a long way from the bat, gave the impression of being an outsider looking in. The end of his Test career was not far away, hastened by an injury that kept him out of action for much of the remainder of that season.

That Test was one of the most remarkable I have ever experienced. New Zealand, after being bowled out for ninety-seven in the first innings, were asked by Illingworth to score 479 in fourteen hours to win – and they made 440. Indeed, when they had reached 402 for five, I thought we were in for the most astonishing defeat in the history of Test cricket.

This was the first evidence that New Zealand had their best all-round team for some years. Their captain, Bev Congdon, played superbly and when it was all over I got the impression that the New Zealanders felt they would have run us even closer but for two lbw decisions that they considered debatable.

In the next Test, at Lord's, we were outplayed for much of the time and New Zealand have never come closer to beating us. In the end, Keith Fletcher's innings of 178 helped to save the game and, with the West Indies series looming ahead I thought it was ominous that our bowlers were beginning to look exhausted after their efforts in India and Pakistan.

However, we won the final Test at Headingley by an innings and one run, helped when the New Zealand bowlers did not use a rain-affected pitch especially well. In fact, the ball moved around a lot during that series and, with hindsight, we would have preferred to meet the West Indies in the first, damper half of the summer.

With some help from the conditions, our weary bowlers would not have been flayed as they were. But I doubt that we could have changed the course of history against a team of awesome strength and one that was composed mainly of players already taking part in English cricket.

Against the West Indies, especially, we no longer have an advantage in playing at home. They know all about our varying conditions and are skilful enough to learn how to cope with them. It is one of the prices we have to pay for the introduction of overseas players.

They beat us in the first Test by an innings and 158 runs. It was a sad English display, cheered only by the performance of Frank Hayes, who made 106 not out in his first Test match, an innings which seemed especially significant at a time when good middle-order batsmen were in short supply in English cricket.

Unfortunately, Hayes found it impossible to live up to that start and disappeared from the Test scene. I do not know why he fell away because I have always felt he was good enough. Judging by my own early problems I would say his trouble has been one of self-confidence rather than a faulty technique – especially when he struggled in the West Indies – but I still expect to see him make runs for England again.

After that Test defeat John Snow was left out. This came as a surprise to most of us. We regarded it as a big – and avoidable – psychological boost to the West Indies, who had considered him to be the best England bowler at the Oval.

The next Test at Edgbaston, was not particularly enjoyable for players or spectators. There was the much-publicized incident between umpire Arthur Fagg and the West Indies captain Rohan Kanhai, tediously slow over rates by both sides and when it ended in a draw we moved on to Lord's all too aware that the public – and the game's image – deserved something far better.

Alas, only one team provided it. The West Indies beat us by an innings and 226 runs. There had been only one heavier defeat in Test History for England – by Australia at Brisbane in 1946 – and this one was an all-too-accurate reflection of the widening gulf between the sides. We were, to put it bluntly, murdered!

Yet that game produced, from Bob Willis, one of the best pieces of fast bowling I have ever seen. The pitch had some pace and bounce and as Willis bowled faster and faster, Knott and the close fielders were driven further and further back. Knott said it was one of the fastest spells of bowling he had ever experienced as a wicket-keeper.

Willis, in fact, took the first four wickets, but Greig and Arnold, particularly, looked drained and the West Indies made 652 with Sobers, Kanhai and Julien all scoring hundreds. A bomb scare, which held the game up for eighty-five minutes, helped to keep the West Indies bowlers fresh and it was all over with a day and a half to spare, my own performances in the series having gone into decline with the rest of the team.

Somebody, I suppose, had to take the blame and that proved to be the end of Illingworth's reign as captain. In that series I had seen him look helpless for the first time, powerless to cut off the avalanche of runs.

He was the best captain I have played under, a fine tactician and a man who, even when things were going wrong, always seemed to have something up his sleeve . . . except against the West Indies. I doubt if any other captain would have been more successful under the circumstances.

Ironically, I felt that in some ways Illingworth had become a victim of his own skill as a captain, because at a time when we were not over-blessed with great players his leadership had held the England team together, camouflaged some weaknesses and brought some success, not least in regaining the Ashes.

At the back of my mind I felt that the humiliation handed us by the West Indies had been coming for some time. We could not disguise the difference in class, especially as we came face to face with their magnificent batsmen on beautiful batting surfaces at a time when our own bowlers were looking decidedly world-weary.

Since my early days in the England team, when Graveney, Barrington and company were present, it has never been really settled. We have always appeared to be rebuilding, trying to unearth fresh talent and there was no way we could match the West Indies.

Meanwhile, there began a great debate about the name of Illingworth's successor. I had it on good authority that Lewis would have been invited to return and take the party to the West Indies if he had been fit enough to play for Glamorgan, while Illingworth himself said that if asked to nominate his replacement he would choose either Boycott or Greig.

Greig, of course, has now acceded to the throne, but many people have asked me – and still do – about Boycott. I would have been happy to play under him and to give him 100 per cent support, but he has always been a law unto himself and no doubt the powers-that-be considered this. Even so, if Boycott had stuck by the England team, it would have been hard to ignore his claims by now.

Among other names mentioned were those of Colin Cowdrey

and Mike Brearley. The selectors obviously felt that to return to Cowdrey would be a retrograde step, though as things turned out his quality as a batsman would have been invaluable to us in the West Indies.

I had played under Brearley on the under-25 tour to Pakistan and in the past few years have been increasingly impressed by his ability as captain of Middlesex. Whether the selectors had doubts about him as a batsman at Test level I do not know.

When Mike Denness was appointed it was something of a surprise. He had been vice-captain in India and Pakistan and if he had not been outstandingly successful neither had he been a total failure, but he had been bypassed for the Tests that summer despite scoring a lot of runs early on.

Now he found himself with the huge responsibility of taking MCC to the West Indies. This is always a hard tour, but now, coming as it did so soon after our comprehensive defeat at home, it began to look impossibly difficult.

If Denness was concerned, he did not show it. He was clearly delighted to have the chance, but on the January morning that we flew from Heathrow to Barbados I doubt if any of us realized that in the next eighteen months Mike Denness would have one of the roughest rides that any England captain can have experienced.

5

A High Score in Jamaica . . .

My biggest Test innings – we go one down in the series – bouncers and no action by the umpires – how I thought I had thrown the Test away – we begin the great escape – a large brandy and why I needed it – I am dubbed 'King of Kingston'

As our aircraft glided in low over the Caribbean to land at Kingston, Jamaica, on a sunny morning in February 1974, I glanced around at my colleagues in the MCC party. It was not hard to read their thoughts. They were probably as depressing as my own.

Still uppermost in our minds was the first Test match against the West Indies in Port of Spain, Trinidad, which we had lost by seven wickets. From a personal point of view it had been a satisfactory one because I had made 174, which was my highest score for England and in the eyes of many people my best innings in terms of quality, also.

With Geoff Boycott I had shared in an opening partnership of 209, a record for England in the West Indies, and after our poor performance in the first innings we had reached a situation on the fourth day when we were not only in a position to save the game, but possibly even win it.

Unfortunately, our batting underwent one of those unaccountable collapses that can happen even in Test cricket. At lunch we were 315 for one, but we contrived to lose seven wickets in the afternoon session and with them went all our hopes.

We had, of course, been outclassed by the West Indies in the home series the previous summer. Now we were already one down, mindful of the vast difference in quality between the two teams, and my first visit to this exotic part of the world had got off to a dismal start.

On the drive from the airport to our hotel, with the splendour of the Blue Mountains in the background contrasting with the shanty towns and their endless rows of houses of unbelievable squalor, I reflected that we would now have a real struggle on our hands to level the series.

We also knew that conditions for the second Test would be different. In Port of Spain the ball had at first moved off the seam and swung, then it had turned. Now we were moving to Sabina Park, which used to be known as one of the fastest pitches anywhere in the world.

Like others throughout the world, however, it has become slower. I did not play in the match against Jamaica, but it was easy to see that this was a beautiful batting surface. With its gentle pace and reliable, even bounce it was the best we saw in the West Indies.

The Jamaica game is, perhaps, best remembered for an incident involving Geoff Arnold and Lawrence Rowe at the start of Jamaica's second innings. I was fielding substitute at the time and as I saw it Rowe glanced Arnold down the legside off the face of the bat.

Bob Taylor, the wicketkeeper, threw himself full length and was actually horizontal and still airborne when he caught the ball one handed. It was a great catch by any standards and a wonderful piece of cricket. Unfortunately, the umpire did not see it as I saw it and he gave Rowe not out.

Within a few moments the crowd was in uproar and we had an unfortunate 'incident' on our hands. Arnold stood there, clearly upset, and I could see his point of view. Bowlers work hard to take wickets in the West Indies and here he had apparently got a star player out without scoring.

But he allowed the episode to unsettle him and he was foolish to start bowling a series of bouncers at Rowe, who is a fine hooker and on that mild pitch helped himself to one boundary after another. Fortunately for us, Rowe made only forty-one and the incident was soon over, which was as well, for we had enough problems with players who were out of form and short of confidence.

We batted only moderately after winning the toss in the Test and our total of 353 was much smaller than we should have made on such a perfect pitch. Once again the West Indies left us far behind, though some of their batting tactics seemed a little strange once they had overhauled our total.

We thought they would then flay our bowling, but they soft-pedalled. Not that we minded of course. In the burning sun we were happy to contain them, though looking back it seems to me that if the West Indies had accelerated when we were at their mercy they would have won the match, regardless of our efforts later.

When we went in again we were 230 runs behind with ten hours left and we were up against it from the start. Boycott and myself were greeted by a barrage of bouncers. I would say we received at least three an over, but in the Caribbean this type of bowling appears to be accepted.

Certainly, no word was spoken to the bowlers – Keith Boyce and Bernard Julien – and Boycott and I had to try to sort things out for ourselves. In that first hour they gave us hell and Boycott was caught at the wicket off his glove off a really awkward bouncer from Boyce.

I had made only a few runs when I survived a strong appeal for a similar catch. As I have said earlier, the ball may have brushed my glove, but in my confused frame of mind I could not be certain and was happy to leave the verdict to the umpire who rejected the appeal.

As the bouncers continued to come, I suddenly found myself playing the hook shot. It was not normally a stroke I had played with much confidence before, but now, encouraged by the even bounce, the desire to counter-attack and the fact that there were many fielders close to the bat, I went for the stroke.

Looking at the scoreboard, I was surprised to find I had made twenty-four in no time at all. Then I came to my senses. As Kanhai moved men out to patrol the boundary, I realized it was time to tighten up and eliminate risks.

John Jameson, at the other end, had other ideas. He is a compulsive hooker and when he played the stroke against yet another bouncer from Boyce the ball ballooned off a top edge and soared into the crowd for six over third man!

As Kanhai stood and glared at him, John, never one to be

overawed, just beamed down the pitch at me and shouted: 'Well, that's one place they can't put a fielder.' He was out, soon afterwards, trying to hit over the top. Throughout the tour Jameson, I felt, tried too consciously to live up to his reputation as a powerful hitter.

That was not the end of our problems. Denness went next, unluckily given out caught off bat and pad, although it turned out he had in fact jabbed his bat against his boot as he played forward. By then I had managed to settle in enough to keep putting the bad balls away to the boundary, so that the bowlers were not entirely in control, but then came a dreadful period when I thought I had presented the Test match to the West Indies single-handed.

I ran out both Frank Hayes and Alan Knott! First, I pushed the ball into the covers where, of course, Clive Lloyd was fielding and called Hayes for a quick single. He never had a chance and after Lloyd had swooped to pick up and throw in all in one movement I knew it must have been a bad call because Hayes is one of the quickest runners between the wickets in the game. If he could not get home, no one could.

The collapse continued when Lance Gibbs got an off-break to turn enough to squeeze through a gap between bat and pad and bowl Tony Greig. It was one of the few balls that turned sharply during the entire match but the sight of it did nothing to encourage us.

It needs only one ball to turn to make you apprehensive and start looking for every ball to do something. Kanhai was now using every tactic in the book to pressurize us and if I have any excuse for running out Knott, which is doubtful, it was because I was concentrating so hard.

In fact, I was so engrossed with the battle for survival that I had hardly realized it was Knott who had joined me. Once again I called for a run to cover and once again Lloyd threw down the stumps. I can still hear Knott's anguished cry of 'Oh, no!' as he realized he would not make it.

We were then 258 for six, only twenty-eight runs ahead and with more than a day to survive. The realization that if I were to get out now there was an angry team waiting in the dressing-room to discuss my running between the wickets made me more determined than ever to survive.

Derek Underwood appeared next, as nightwatchman, and

I immediately walked down the pitch and asked him to protect me. By then I had passed my century and it may seem strange that a batsman who had been at the wicket as long as I had should ask a tail-ender for 'protection'.

But it may not be generally realized that the job of a cricketing nightwatchman is to look after his partner as well as protect later batsmen. In that respect Underwood did a fine job, calmly playing out the last over and leaving me – very, very tired – to lean on my bat and watch admiringly from the other end.

As I walked off, saturated with perspiration and mentally drained after the tension of those four incident-packed hours, I wanted nothing more than a cold drink, a hot bath and sleep. At least, I thought, I am still there for tomorrow.

Even then our chances of saving the game seemed remote. After all, we were only a handful of runs ahead with only Chris Old, Pat Pocock and Bob Willis to bat. The new ball was due, too. How could we escape?

In the dressing-room the atmosphere was gloomy, naturally, but my attempts to apologize about the two run-out episodes were cut short. The rest of the team did not want me to lose any sleep over my mistakes. After all, I still had a chance to put things right!

The rest of that day is a blur in my memory. The next thing I knew was Alan Knott, my room-mate, waking me up and saying with typical optimism: 'Come on, you've got to bat all day today!'

On the way to the ground the adrenalin began to flow. There seemed to be more spectators than ever. Doubtless they were all there for the kill. Inside Sabina Park everywhere was ablaze with colour and there was a buzz of laughter, chatter and excitement, but it died away to an eerie silence the moment that Underwood and I reached the middle.

Kanhai did not take the new ball immediately, but relied on the spin of Gibbs and Barrett. It nearly paid off, too, because before I had played myself in again I was dropped at backward short leg by Sobers off Gibbs.

I hit the ball hard off the middle of the bat and I suppose you would not class it as a chance in any form of cricket other than a Test match. But they are the sort of catches which win and lose matches and Sobers was one man who could sometimes catch them.

Fortunately for England and for me, this one was just a little too sharp for him. Soon we had the new ball to contend with and Boyce was again an awkward proposition as he again dug it in regularly short of a length, but Underwood got right behind the line and fended everything off very bravely.

Once he walked down the pitch and asked me: 'How am I doing?' 'Very well,' I said. 'Oh, am I really?' he answered, and walked back looking very pleased. I suspect that innings gave him almost as much pleasure as some of his bowling performances.

I tried to manipulate the bowling to take as much of the strike as possible, but eventually Sobers came on to bowl in his quicker style while the ball was still new and he had Underwood caught behind. He had survived another seventy-five minutes, but we were only forty-one runs ahead with three wickets left and most of the day before us.

It must have been long odds on a West Indies victory, but the rest of our batsmen had caught the mood of defiance. Chris Old withstood another barrage of bouncers to stay for a hundred minutes while we added another seventy-two runs and Pat Pocock, although scoring only four runs himself, survived for another valuable eighty-five minutes.

By tea I had left behind my previous highest first-class score, 192 against Lancashire, and had reached 200 for the first time in my life. More importantly, the match was almost saved, though there was still a slight chance of defeat if we lost our remaining wickets quickly.

The dressing-room atmosphere was much more relaxed this time. As I staggered in, bedraggled and almost too weary to make the change of clothing I needed, someone shouted: 'Doesn't he look just like a sack of — ?' I could not argue and 'Sacka' has been my nickname to the England players ever since.

I have always made a point of not drinking during a match, but when I was offered a large brandy during the interval I felt, for once, that the situation justified it. I was so drained of energy and struggling so much to maintain my concentration that some kind of stimulant was needed.

After tea the West Indies appeared for the final session several minutes late, as if to suggest that they had abandoned hope of winning and did not share our worries that we could lose if we were all out quickly. They were right, as it happened, for by the time Pocock was out we were 162 ahead and safe.

Bob Willis came next and Kanhai showed his feelings by putting on his occasional bowlers. Even then Willis was anxious. 'For Christ's sake, don't get out now – see it right through,' he said to me. I can recall Bob taking the last two overs and Kanhai coming across to shake my hand as we walked off, but much of that day is now just a vague but pleasant memory.

That night, sleep eluded me. I could not stop replaying the innings in my mind . . . ball after ball, stroke after stroke. I thought fleetingly of some of the great players of the past who had made bigger scores in Test matches and had an even greater respect for them.

Next morning came a batch of congratulatory telegrams, followed by letters in their hundreds from all parts of England. I answered them all personally, though it took me to the end of the tour to do it. This was around the time of the General Election in England and the *Birmingham Mail* published a cartoon which said: 'Amiss for Prime Minister', while their back-page headline said: 'Amiss – King of Kingston'.

During the celebrations that night, when I narrowly avoided being thrown fully clothed into the hotel swimming pool (Tony Greig and our manager Donald Carr were not so lucky), my thoughts frequently turned to the days when I had struggled to become established, to that infamous 'pair' at Old Trafford and to the people who had never lost faith in me. It helped me to keep things in proportion. It was fine to save a Test match with a big, unbeaten innings, but it must be better, I felt, to win one by making a large score against the clock.

But the mood of the MCC party had been given a tremendous lift by our escape. We were still one down in the series, of course, but we now felt more confident, capable of playing much better and doing ourselves justice.

6

. . . and a Turnabout in Trinidad

Our first meeting with Roberts – why we made a disastrous change in the batting order – Rowe hits a triple Test century – Greig shows his all-round talents – Boycott hits 99 and is criticized – the most important Test I have known – the qualities which saved the series

Of all the island paradises in the West Indies – and there are many – Antigua comes high on my personal list. It has 365 beaches, one for each day of the year if you are so inclined, and I found it the perfect place to unwind after the great escape in Jamaica.

I appreciated the lush, tranquil setting of our hotel, with its view over the Caribbean, more than most, because I was still physically and mentally exhausted. My ten-hour innings in Kingston seemed firmly embedded in my mind and at all hours of the day and night I was still either playing strokes or looking anxiously at the scoreboard.

Under the circumstances I should have rested instead of playing in our game against the Leeward Islands. I was given the option and chose to miss the next match, against Barbados, believing that a break just before the third Test would be more beneficial.

In fact, both matches were played on pitches that were too lively, the sort that can upset the batsman who is in form as well as be the despair of the man trying to find it.

The pitch at St John's, Antigua is, I gather, normally a beauty to bat on, but ours was highly unpredictable in bounce, not the type I would have chosen for our first meeting with Andy Roberts. It is prepared by convicts from the local prison and on the first morning Mike Denness casually asked one of them how long he had been rolling it, expecting the usual answer of five minutes or something similar.

'Two years, sir,' was the cheerful reply. 'And another ten to do!'

Though the match against the Islanders was drawn, it was lively enough. So was the next game against Barbados, where we produced one of our worst performances of the tour and lost by ten wickets to a team lacking their two leading players, Sobers and Boyce.

In my opinion the pitches in the West Indies are the best in the world for batting – I have played in Tests everywhere except South Africa – because they are hard and true. They are virtually grassless so that the shine disappears from the ball quickly and the spinners are always involved, making it a better game.

The pitch where we met our defeat at Bridgetown, however, was not one of them. It was a recently laid one, underprepared no doubt because attention was concentrated on the Test strip, and after a spell of wet weather was lively indeed.

Yet we still went into the Test with a reasonable degree of confidence. We believed we could hold the West Indies, strong as they were, in the next two Tests and then stood a chance of winning over six days on another turning pitch at Port of Spain.

That theory turned out to be correct, but we had more problems at Bridgetown where we made an experiment with the batting order that proved disastrous. It was decided by the tour selection committee (Mike Denness, Donald Carr, Tony Greig, Alan Knott and Geoff Boycott) that Boycott should vacate his number one position and drop down the order.

There were two reasons for this. One was that Boycott could give the middle order some of the fibre that had been missing. The other was that Geoff himself had not been in the best of form and might achieve more if protected from the steep bounce that had troubled him in the previous game.

Boycott himself was not entirely in agreement with the idea, but he accepted in the best interests of the team. Nor were we in total agreement about John Jameson batting at number three. Both Bob Willis and myself, his county team-mates, felt that as John was in the team he might as well go in first with me and, hopefully, we would see the shine off the new ball.

Jameson is a natural hooker and puller, at his best when the ball is new and therefore bouncing more, and you have to let him have his head. Like Australia's Keith Stackpole, he might need some luck at times but on his day he is capable of taking an attack to pieces very quickly.

Not here, though. Kanhai put us in on another lively pitch, Roberts bowled very fast on his first appearance for the West Indies and none of the first four batsmen, myself included, were very comfortable. We soon found ourselves with our backs to the wall again at sixty-eight for four.

But as the pitch lost its early life, Tony Greig and Alan Knott staged another rescue with a partnership of 163 that enabled England to make 395. It was significant for both players. Knott's assured innings ended a spell when he had struggled to make runs for England; Greig's innings of 148 was only the start of a tremendous all-round performance.

Our eventual total represented a good recovery, but we knew it was again only modest on a pitch that was now perfect. Exactly how modest was illustrated by Lawrence Rowe, who scored 302, only the eleventh triple century in Test cricket, out of 596 for eight declared.

I had an idea Rowe was about to produce something special when early in his innings he hooked a short-pitched ball from Bob Willis flat and hard over square leg for six. It was one of the finest strokes I have ever seen.

Rowe continued to roll out one glorious shot after another and went on to make the highest individual score for the West Indies against England. He dominated the innings so much that another century by Alvin Kallicharran passed almost unnoticed and no matter what we tried the West Indies seemed to score at around four runs an over.

Looking at Rowe, I found it hard to understand why he had never before played a substantial Test-match innings outside his native Jamaica. He seemed to have everything: a splendid technique, a good temperament and plenty of time to play his strokes.

From our point of view the most significant aspect of this Test was the bowling of Greig. He sent down forty-six overs and most of them were the medium-paced off-spinners which he had been developing in the nets and which he now tried in the middle for the first time.

They have since become important to the balance of the England attack, but at that stage Tony, of course, did not possess the accuracy he discovered later and it was not easy to set a field for him; but from his vast height he made the ball bounce and sometimes turn and so began a new chapter in English cricket history.

Greig took six wickets for 164 and thus became the first England player to score a century and take five wickets in a Test match. In addition, he held a brilliant slip catch to dismiss Sobers for nought – the first time he had failed to score in a Test on his own ground – and so was making his presence felt in all departments of the game as usual.

Life, however, was not so good for some of us. Our re-arranged batting order again failed in the second innings, when we needed 201 to make the West Indies bat again. After a long stint in the field we were weary and, losing four wickets for forty runs, found ourselves in the middle of another crisis.

But by now the team had acquired a certain resilience and determination and this time it was Keith Fletcher and Alan Knott who revived the innings. Knott made his second half-century of the match, Fletcher was unbeaten with 129, an innings which was a masterpiece of concentration and patience, and, almost unbelievably, we had escaped again.

We were delighted to have saved the game and if you are tempted to think we were letting our emotions and judgement get carried away, I feel it is worth pointing out that we were competing against a team who were probably the best in the world at that time.

That West Indies side had everything. With its balance, class and depth of batting, quality of fast bowling and most types of spin, not to mention the best all-rounder the game has ever produced, it must have been one of the most powerful Test teams of all time.

So, far from being despondent, we were well satisfied that we were still in with a chance of saving the series. Nor did the fourth Test at Georgetown, Guyana, harm our prospects. The match was ruined by rain and drawn, but by batting first and scoring 448 we were able to put the West Indies under pressure for the first time in the series.

Even before a ball was bowled there were signs that all was not well in the West Indies' camp. Sobers withdrew from their team at the last minute, saying he needed a rest, and this was a bigger blow to the West Indies than might have been realized at the time. True, his all-round contribution to the series had fallen away, but the very name of Sobers in a West Indian team had come to mean something far more than just runs and wickets. His presence used to reassure the others.

We were pleasantly surprised, too, to find that Roberts had not been chosen, despite the undoubted promise of his performance in Barbados, and altogether the West Indies went into this match very defensively. Before lunch Lloyd and Foster were bowling with the field pushed back, even though they had dismissed Boycott cheaply.

I made a hundred, which I found hard going in view of the defensive fields, and was annoyed with myself when I was caught off a glove trying to hook. Greig also made a century that was full of dazzling strokes and when the West Indies batted the ball turned just enough to make them uneasy.

Rain, however, put an end to all the speculation and we were soon on our way back to Port of Spain for the decisive final Test which, with the series still undecided, could, of course, go into a sixth day if necessary. Though my own contribution was not as big as I would have liked, I doubt if I will ever play in a more important match.

From start to finish it was governed by tension. It seesawed back and forth, with both teams thinking they had it won, and there were any number of turning points. We won a vital toss, we kept our heads better than the West Indies at crucial moments, but the entire game hinged on the performance of Geoff Boycott and Tony Greig.

By his own standards, Boycott had enjoyed only a moderate series but this was an ideal challenge for him. The pitch was uneven in bounce but time was on our side, we had set ourselves a target of about 350 runs and Boycott was able to graft his way to ninety-nine before he was brilliantly caught by Murray.

In view of the circumstances it was surprising to learn later that his innings had been criticized for its slowness in some English newspapers. But its value was apparent to us, especially as our last six wickets went down for only sixty-three runs and we were almost a hundred short of our self-imposed target.

The West Indies, indeed, led us by thirty-eight on the first innings, thanks to Rowe, who, in contrast to his effervescent stroke-play in Barbados and in deference to the pitch, got his head down as Boycott had done and scored his third century of the series.

But neither Rowe's century nor the West Indies lead concerned us too much because we were thrilled by Greig's bowling. Only a month or so after experimenting in the nets with his off-spinners he took eight wickets for eighty-six runs – against the world's strongest batting side. It was a remarkable performance, not only because it was the first time that Greig had bowled a team out in his slower style but because the pitch, though turning slowly and unevenly, was not entirely unplayable as other spinners discovered.

No, much of the credit went to Greig himself. He made the ball bounce again and he turned it, but, just as importantly, he took some of his wickets with the ball that went straight on. And, as ever, he looked as if he expected to take a wicket with every ball he bowled.

Certainly, his performance must have sown a few seeds of doubt in the minds of the West Indies batsmen when, after another fine innings by Boycott (112 this time), they began the last day at thirty for none, needing 226 to win. Frankly, we thought we had not made enough runs and that West Indies had only to bat normally and sensibly to win, but they were in an unusual situation. They had dominated the series and now they could see they were in danger of having their triumph snatched from them at the last possible moment.

In the end it was, but only after a day in which the match tilted dramatically one way, then the other. When Rowe and Fredericks put on sixty-three for the first wicket, for instance, I did not give much for our chances.

Then the West Indies lost three wickets for two runs and everything changed. One of them, Rowe, fell to Jack Birkenshaw, who in a match when England had four spin bowlers available bowled only eighteen overs, but this was an important contribution.

Fredericks was run out, Kallicharran incongruously rounded off a successful series by completing a 'pair' and then Greig dismissed both Kanhai and Lloyd, either of whom might have won the match single-handed if they had settled in.

So it went on. Sobers, playing with ominous calm and certainty of judgement, was suddenly deceived by a ball that Underwood cunningly flighted. It was the first time Underwood had ever dismissed Sobers and what a moment to do it!

Indeed, Underwood's tremendous accuracy in closing up the opposite end to Greig was another factor in our win, but even then the drama continued with Murray, Boyce and Inshan Ali all providing stubborn resistance. In the end we had to take the new ball and there was an hour left when Arnold bowled Gibbs to give us victory by twenty-six runs.

Afterwards, I felt as if a great weight had been lifted from my shoulders. Then I looked at one of the men responsible, Tony Greig, whose eight wickets in an innings and thirteen in the match were the best for England since Jim Laker's nineteen against Australia in 1956. He had also beaten Trevor Bailey's seven for thirty-four as the best figures for England against the West Indies.

The emergence of Greig as a genuine Test all-rounder was one of the factors which helped us to save the series. Yet, at a time when England were not over-blessed with great cricketers, the old-fashioned qualities of courage and endeavour had also helped us to survive against opponents who, man for man, were far more gifted than we were.

7

Inconsistency at Edgbaston

The quality missing from Warwickshire cricket – why we have never won the John Player League – did the BBC cost us a Gillette Cup victory? – how Kanhai has changed – what the Australian said to A. C. Smith – the player whose loss was a tragic waste of talent

No matter how much he travels around the world, every English cricketer never loses sight of the importance of his own county club. It is, after all, the one which gave him a start in life and which pays his wages. In my case I have been fortunate to spend all my career with such a progressive county as Warwickshire.

At Edgbaston no player, whether he is an old professional or a youngster on the ground staff, can complain that his needs are not met. As befits one of the world's finest grounds, it has everything. You can laze in the sauna bath, work out in the gymnasium or practice on three different types of pitches in the indoor school.

Thanks to their supporters' club, Warwickshire have not felt cricket's financial problems as severely as some counties. From humble beginnings in a little room under the scoreboard it has developed into a huge money-spinning organization which helps not only Warwickshire but other clubs at all levels.

Behind the scenes we have a sympathetic relationship between players and committee, which helps to eliminate the type of problems which seem to crop up elsewhere, and a first-class administrator in Leslie Deakins.

I know of no one who does more for cricket. In summer he often works at his desk until ten in the evening. In winter he spends five nights a week speaking at cricketing functions, but he will always find time to talk to a player with a problem.

So we have a fine, well-organized county club which we are all proud to represent. But all this would be meaningless without success and although the Warwickshire team has achieved some, there are those who think we have not done as much as Edgbaston and the Warwickshire members and supporters deserve.

Though it has a huge population, Birmingham is not a cricket-loving city. The hearts of most people seem to belong to Aston Villa or Birmingham City. But, then, I believe we have generally been too inconsistent to attract the large crowds a ground like ours needs.

Obviously this was what prompted the club to sign players like Bob Willis and our overseas stars. Even so, I still feel we have too often been a team of individuals, some of them admittedly brilliant, whose combined efforts ought to have achieved more.

To be fair, in my time we have won the county championship once, finished runners-up twice and we have appeared in four Gillette Cup finals, winning two of them. Yet with the talent at our disposal is that enough?

When you consider that at times we have fielded as many as ten Test players – with the odd man out someone as talented as Norman McVicker – you will see what I mean. We have, of course, suffered from Test-match calls but I do not regard that as a conclusive answer.

We have, it is true, played more colourful and attractive cricket than some counties I could name. We have risked defeat to bring dying matches back to life. But we have also lacked application – or perhaps killer instinct is a better description.

I am not suggesting our methods have been entirely wrong. We have needed possibly to tilt the balance slightly the other way, but with Warwickshire there never seems to be a happy medium: we are either brilliant or bloody awful.

For instance, if there is one trophy we should have won by now it is the John Player League. This competition, with its emphasis on batting and with many bowlers handicapped by their limited run-ups, looks ideal for a team like ours. Our failure to do so has concerned our committee because this is

D

the competition that attracts the crowds and makes money. But we never seem capable of batting *and* bowling well in the same match and the fact that we have no genuine all-rounder means that we cannot improvise if a bowler has an off-day. We are also, let us admit it, not exactly a brilliant fielding side.

Nevertheless, many counties would settle for what we *have* achieved. And I was particularly delighted to play in the Warwickshire team that won the county championship in 1972, especially as we had gone so close the previous year.

We finished level on points with Surrey, who took the title because they had won more matches. No county in history had ever been so close to the championship pennant without winning it; in previous years teams level on points shared the title.

We were not, perhaps, ideally equipped to win that year. I recall Alan Smith writing at the time that in the opinion of most observers it was 'a sustained effort of improvisation that almost succeeded in covering up known deficiencies. If Warwickshire had scraped the necessary point to win the title it would have been the most outrageous larceny since the Great Train Robbery.'

That year we were also beaten by Kent in a Gillette Cup semi-final at Canterbury. Rain had got under the covers overnight and the match was virtually decided on the toss, which we lost, because the team bowling first would have to use a wet ball and then bat when the pitch was getting more difficult as it dried.

Fair enough. You have to accept the rub of the green, even in one-day cricket, but what annoyed us at the time was the fact that on the other side of the square was a perfectly dry pitch which could have been used. We had to play on the wet one because the BBC's television cameras were already in position and could not be moved!

So we began the 1972 season convinced that fate had not been too kind to us. Our view that we were capable of winning something was strengthened by the fact that Alvin Kallicharran had qualified to play for us, Deryck Murray had joined us from Nottinghamshire and Bob Willis would be available halfway through the season after leaving Surrey.

In fact, we won the title in some comfort without losing a match. Kanhai hit eight centuries and made 1600 runs, but our bowlers did more than they were given credit for at the time. Winning the toss only four times – and we put the opposition in twice – seemed to help and we won many matches against the clock.

Only twice were we in danger of defeat. First on a badly worn pitch at Leicester we managed to hold out. Then on a rain-affected one at Bramall Lane, Sheffield, only the weather saved us from certain defeat by Yorkshire.

But I shall always remember this match for one of the funniest episodes I have ever seen on a cricket field. Certainly it was the only time I have been dismissed for nought and have walked back to the pavilion paralysed with laughter.

On the second morning Jameson and I began the innings after week-end rain had left the ground saturated and hardly fit for play. Tony Nicholson opened the bowling and before a run was scored I pushed him into the covers and called for a single.

Jameson launched his massive figure down the greasy pitch, got halfway and then plunged forward on to his face. Covered from head to toe in mud, he remained sprawled across the pitch despite his frantic efforts to scramble to his feet and, seeing this, I tried to pull up and turn back.

Instead, I went sliding down the pitch as if I was wearing skis, heading straight for the prostrate body of my wretched partner who was still lying there, cursing to himself. While all this was happening, Colin Johnson, fielding at cover, swooped for the ball, sensing an easy run out, but as he collected it he too slid on to his backside.

Meanwhile, I skidded to a halt and headed for home. Johnson staggered to his feet and threw to my end where David Bairstow, who had, of course, been standing back, charged up to the stumps to collect the ball. But he also slipped and came hurtling towards the stumps on his backside, like a child on a toboggan.

Somehow, as he reached the stumps, Bairstow stuck a hand in the air, caught Johnson's throw, broke the wicket as he went past and continued his merry way for several more yards, leaving me comfortably run out and, like the entire Yorkshire team, helpless with laughter.

It is now history that we went on to win the title, but what of the players who helped to do it? I thought a little insight into the qualities of some of my colleagues, on and off the field, would be revealing, so I have compiled this brief dossier on Warwickshire players of 1972 and earlier.

John Jameson. He has a marvellous attitude for an opening batsman in that he does not think anyone can bowl – including Dennis Lillee! Indeed, I recall one memorable innings in which Lillee bowled bouncer after bouncer at Jameson and he struck them over extra cover.

John is a fine, confident player and an extremely generous colleague with a lovely sense of humour. On MCC's tour of the West Indies he missed a few matches and enjoyed the social life. On his return, when an umpire asked him what he would like (referring to his guard), he replied: 'A rum and coke, please!'

John Whitehouse. He bats with an open stance like Jim Parks used to and we all thought this would make him vulnerable outside the off stump, but he has proved a sound player, though he has been under pressure to live up to an exceptional first season.

As a qualified accountant, he does not depend on county cricket for a living, but if he could give the game his full attention he could become a high-class player.

Rohan Kanhai. His ability to 'explode', to do the unexpected, has won us a lot of matches and I have learned from watching him. He has disciplined himself to bat like an English player and now makes massive scores after the dazzling, but all-too-brief fifties and sixties of his early years.

He is capable of destroying any attack on good pitches, but one of the best innings I have ever seen came when he made a century against Underwood on an unreliable one at Gravesend. He plays bridge as flamboyantly as he plays cricket – if you are his partner and you make a mistake you soon hear about it!

Alvin Kallicharran. He is regarded by the Warwickshire team as the best Test batsman in the world today. He is quick on his feet, beautifully balanced, sees the ball early and hits it hard off front or back foot. Last summer a surfeit of Test cricket seemed to have taken its toll and there were times when he looked as though he would fall asleep at the wicket. I hope two more series last winter have not left him even more exhausted.

Mike Smith. He looks aloof and it can take time to get to know him, but for years he dominated the conversation in our dressing-room. Absent-minded, but a great player, especially of spin. I once saw him make 180 against Sam Cook, John Mortimore and David Allen on a turning pitch to win a match we should have lost.

He may go down in cricket history as the man who invented the 'lap' stroke from outside the off stump through midwicket or square leg. Indeed, throughout his career he was a strong onside player and to him the offside was known as 'the cissy side'.

Deryck Murray. He has proved invaluable to us in an era when it has become increasingly important for wicketkeepers to make their share of runs. Mainly a back-foot player, a fine hooker and one of the nicest people in the game. Not a showman behind the stumps, but extremely competent without reaching the highest class and a more than useful leg-spinner, too.

Alan Smith. Remarkable as a wicketkeeper who was equally serviceable as a bowler and who, indeed, discarded his pads to do the hat-trick against Essex. His peculiar walk down the pitch, the subject of many impersonations, was due to arthritis in his kneecaps and once in Australia a spectator shouted at him: 'No wonder you made a duck, Smith – you walk like one.' It may not be generally known that he was frequently the man behind the move of many star players to Edgbaston.

David Brown. He is still a fine bowler, though obviously not as fast as he used to be, and has battled his way through all sorts of injuries. He figured in the most remarkable real-life romance I have ever heard of when at a race meeting in the West Indies, all the MCC players put their money on the only woman jockey. She won, David had the job of expressing their thanks – and she is now his wife.

Norman McVicker. Widely known as 'the Gentleman Cricketer' because of his habit of applauding anybody who hits him for four or six. He has never been heard to swear; when he bowls a bad ball he mutters 'Stone the crows' quietly to himself. It was a pity he left Edgbaston, though he has found success with Leicestershire, because there would still have been a place for him if he had stayed.

Lance Gibbs. He found it hard to adjust to English pitches, especially wet ones, and he could never drift the ball away like most English-born off-spinners. Still a magnificent bowler, though, with a lovely loop and many skilfully disguised variations of pace.

He would still be playing for Warwickshire but for being offered a coaching post in Guyana and I back him to run Fred Trueman's record 307 Test-match wickets close before he eventually retires.

Bob Willis. He has an excellent fast bowler's temperament because he can generate hostility towards the batsman without losing his own self-control. His main asset is his height and he extracts bounce rather than pronounced movement. He has been troubled a lot by injury, but the way he came back towards the end of last season suggested he will again be a force in 1976.

Bob Barber. He became a changed player after leaving Lancashire, developing from a defensive batsman to a glorious stroke-maker. He always appeared to be supremely confident about batting, but not so sure about his leg-spinners, and often he had to be persuaded to bowl. It was a tragic waste of talent when business commitments took him away from county cricket.

Tom Cartwright. He began as an opening batsman in Warwickshire's second team and then became one of the most respected medium-pace bowlers in the game. Indeed, it is not exaggeration to call him a great bowler in English conditions, with his magnificent action and superb rhythm.

In his early days he could bowl the outswinger and inswinger with no detectable change of action and I have stood for hours at slip not knowing which way the ball would go. I have met only one batsman (Colin Cowdrey) who claimed he did know.

8

In a Trance at the Oval

Did the Press give England enough credit? – the man who pays out when I make runs – leaky covers and a Pakistani protest – was this a diplomatic draw? – a century and illness at the Oval – why I agreed to be hypnotized

When the 1974 cricket season in England began I had never felt as confident in my life. After my successes in the West Indies, I began the summer by playing better than at any other time, hit 195 against Middlesex in my first championship match and enjoyed our comprehensive victory over India in the first Test series of the year.

It was, as we expected, a rather gentler experience than our tour of the Caribbean and after all the pressure and problems involved there it was good to play in a series where everything went so much our way, though to some people it all seemed *too* easy.

Some of the Press, for instance, appeared to go out of their way to sympathize with the Indians because they encountered pitches that did not suit their bowlers. They seemed to have forgotten that we had lost our last two series against them, and therefore had a lot to prove.

When we were beaten by India we were written off as not good enough. Now we proved much the better side and did not get the credit we deserved. We took the chance – very rare in a modern Test series – to grind our opponents into the dust and because we took control so early in the series the Indians were perhaps made to look a worse team than they actually were.

It is worthwhile, in view of the way that series was received, examining briefly the relationship between cricketers and the Press, particularly at Test level. This can be very delicate, especially on tour and even more so if England are doing badly.

The last two MCC tours, to the West Indies and Australia, were particularly difficult ones because we were struggling. You expect criticism when you are doing badly, but my view is the less you know the better about what is being written about you and appearing in the newspapers back home.

Unfortunately, on both these tours one of our players was the regular recipient of cuttings of almost everything from the English papers. It became a regular habit of members of the team to spend an evening reading them and becoming more and more depressed – and developing an anti-Press complex – as a result.

I do not mind anyone criticizing my own performances as long as they are constructive about it. There are some members of the Press who can and do write in this manner, but unfortunately there are others whose job it is to seize on an angle. To them, the game is all black and white, with no grey areas in between.

In my early days I took so much criticism from the Press – most of it deserved, I hasten to add, in view of my regular failures – that I gave up reading the papers and tended not to mix with cricket writers. This was not so much out of pique as for thinking they would not want to waste their time talking to a struggling cricketer, anyway.

Since then my outlook has changed. I still rarely read the papers (especially when I know I have played badly!), but I have learned that each individual player should play his part in trying to build up a relationship of mutual trust and respect with the Press, particularly on tour.

So I tend to react to cricket writers on how I find them as people, not because of what they write. I have even played bridge with many of them on various tours and I have been given stick for that at times by my team-mates, I can tell you.

My own up-and-down Test career has also led to a remarkable wager between two members of the Press fraternity. When I was left out of the England team in 1971 John Thicknesse, of the London *Evening Standard*, thought this was the end of my Test career and said so; John Woodcock, of *The Times*, disagreed.

Above: I advance to drive Bishen Bedi.

But *below* although Bedi was one of the Indian bowlers who helped my career, he still took my wicket at Old Trafford in 1974.

Above left: Jeff Thomson. In contrast, a slinging action which is not one for the purist. His remarkable pace is generated by a powerful pair of shoulders. An additional problem for the batsman is that the ball is concealed until very late, making it difficult to pick up.

I duck into a short ball from Lillee which hits me on the shoulder during the third Test at Melbourne, December 1974. We spent a lot of time ducking and weaving on that tour.

Dennis Lillee. He produced one of the fastest spells I have ever faced. Here you can see a beautiful, side-on controlled action as he leaps into the delivery stride and follow through, a perfect example for any youthful fast bowler.

I take a blow on the elbow from a short-pitched ball during the Edgbaston Test 1975. Not much sympathy from the crowd of onlookers, either.

Middlesex's John Murray counts himself unlucky to be caught by me at Edgbaston in 1972, during the match that was a turning point in my career (see page 23).

1975 was not the happiest of seasons for me, but I did achieve the comparatively rare feat of making a century in my benefit match against Kent. Here Alan Knott and Colin Cowdrey look on as I obtain four of the runs off Derek Underwood.

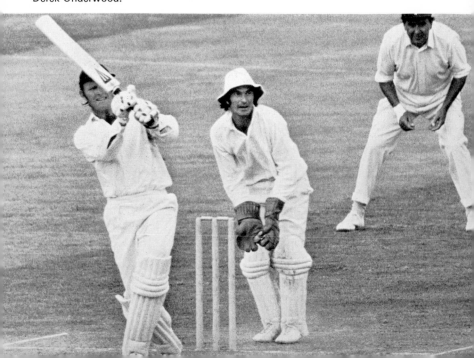

Thicknesse, renowned on the cricket circuit as a betting man who would even gamble on which umpire reached the middle first (and the son of a clergyman, too!), agreed to pay Woodcock 2½p – or sixpence as it was then – for every run over a thousand that I scored for England. Remember that at that stage I had managed only a couple of hundred or so.

Happily, I passed this milestone some time in 1973 and Woodcock started to collect, especially the following year. To show his gratitude, he once took my wife Jill and myself out to dinner subsidized by the proceeds of one innings. I regret that his steady, tax-free income was suddenly cut off in 1975, but only temporarily I hope.

In 1974 – to the delight of Woodcock as well as myself – I averaged ninety-two against India but still finished only fifth in the batting behind David Lloyd, Keith Fletcher, John Edrich and Mike Denness. It was strange that Geoff Boycott's name did not figure in this run glut but he had asked to be left out of the Test team after failing and – as I have said elsewhere – he did not seem to be in the right frame of mind for the job.

Having demolished India, we turned our attention to Pakistan. This, we knew, would be a much tougher series. They had a greater depth of batting, some of it high-class, better seam bowlers and like the West Indians the previous year they had many players familiar to English conditions.

So we expected a battle and we got one, starting with a remarkable match at Headingley where the ball swung around and moved off the seam for the entire game. I cannot recall ever seeing the ball do as much anywhere, especially in a Test match, and there were times when Geoff Arnold was beating the bat with four balls an over.

The humid weather was responsible, although the ball invariably swings a lot at Leeds, and it proved you can have an interesting Test match without conditions being loaded in favour of the bat. Sadly, this one was rained off on the last day with England needing forty-four runs to win with four wickets standing . . . and with both sides strongly fancying their chances. We certainly thought we could do it, with Keith Fletcher still there and with Chris Old, Geoff Arnold, Derek Underwood and Mike Hendrick to back him up. I suppose people will argue for ever about what would have happened.

Similarly, the next Test at Lord's will also be discussed for a long time, especially by the Pakistanis. After winning the toss and taking first use of a beautiful batting pitch they were caught not once but twice by Derek Underwood on a rain-affected one and this time we were certain winners but for the weather.

Under the circumstances, however, it was probably as well that rain intervened. Pakistan, after collapsing from seventy-one for none to 130 for nine declared in their first innings, were bowled out again in their second innings. But the crucial difference was that on the second occasion rain had got under the covers, turning a good pitch into a difficult one.

In the first innings it was just the luck of the game – it rained after play had started and the covers were off. In the second, Pakistan recovered to 173 for three on Saturday night, a lead of thirty-three, but they arrived at the ground on Monday to find that heavy week-end rain had seeped under the covers, something which is very difficult to prevent at Lords' because of the slope.

The result was a pitch that was damp at one end and, of course, perfect for Underwood. Naturally Pakistan protested and we sympathized with their plight. To get caught twice in one match was desperate luck, but having expressed our sympathy we got on with the job of bowling them out.

Our attitude was that every precaution had been taken and had the situation been reversed we would have had to accept it with the minimum of fuss. Underwood took eight for fifty-one to go with his five for twenty in the first innings, earned by a mixture of high-class bowling and some of the peculiar strokes that batsmen tend to play when they are in such a situation. We needed only eighty-seven to win and David Lloyd and myself made twenty-seven of them before the close.

That was as far as we went because it rained again the next day. Naturally, Pakistan were not keen to play and the umpires, Charlie Elliott and David Constant, decided the conditions were unfit, though there were one or two England players who thought that play could have been possible at certain times during the day.

It is not for me to suggest that this might have been an exercise in diplomacy after the controversy over the covers, but it was probably as well that we also suffered from the weather. We would have never heard the last of it if we had won and, indeed,

Pakistan set about us at the Oval as if determined to show what they could do, given a decent batting pitch.

They had that all right and they made 600 for seven. Majid Khan made batting look particularly easy in scoring ninety-eight, Zaheer Abbas hit 240, his second double century against England, Mushtaq contributed seventy-six and when we batted I hit a century myself as England set out to try to save the game.

Yet it was not because of any those innings that I will never forget this Test match. Many people will, because the slowness of the pitch and the nature of the game meant that it became increasingly lacking in incident, except in the pavilion where one member of the England team was hypnotized in the middle of his innings.

That was me. Some strange things have happened to me during my career, but this must surely be the oddest. It was something I never dreamed of at the close of play on Saturday night when I had made 168 not out, as good an innings as I have played for England before or since.

Of course, I never took the bowling to pieces as one or two of the Pakistani batsmen had, but then my brief was different. In view of the huge total we were facing, someone had to bat a long time, to make a big hundred and make sure that we did not follow on. I saw that as my job.

Apart from a run-out escape when I had made 114 and had to hurl myself full length to beat an eighty-yard throw by Aftab Baloch, the substitute, everything went as planned. I walked off sensing that there would be many more runs there for the taking on Monday, but over the week-end I was taken ill with food-poisoning.

I was running a temperature, had a sleepless night on the Sunday and on Monday morning Mike Denness called in a doctor. By then it was raining, so I was not too unhappy at being told to stay in bed, but soon after lunch Mike telephoned to ask me to go to the ground because play was going to start.

When I tentatively resumed my innings, Asif Masood bowled me a half-volley which I eased through the covers. But the pleasure of that stroke was quickly replaced by queasiness in my stomach. My legs felt like jelly and I could not concentrate.

Soon afterwards Sarfraz bowled me a bouncer which I tried

to hook, but I was too early with the stroke and I did not move inside the line. The ball struck my right cheek, leaving only a slight cut, but I was dazed and wobbled around hazily for some moments.

I almost passed out, was revived by smelling salts, decided to carry on and then agreed to go off after almost passing out a second time. In the dressing-room I did pass out and the next morning I got padded up again, although by now the game was safe and I was not going to bat until nine wickets were down.

While I was watching the game and trying to come to terms with an aching jaw and fierce headache, I received a telephone call in the little kiosk just inside the dressing-room. 'I am Mrs —, the hypnotist,' said a voice when I picked up the phone. 'I have been watching you on television. Does your jaw still ache?'

'Not half,' I said. 'I can hardly open my mouth.'

'Very well,' came the reply. 'I am going to hypnotize you over the telephone. I shall tell you that your jaw is all right, you will be able to open it wide when I have finished and you will not feel any pain, nor will you bear any malice against the bowler who hit you. You will go out and continue where you left off on Saturday night, you will score many more runs and you will never worry about being hit again because you are such a good player. . . .'

The look of astonishment on my face caused the dressing-room attendant, and a member of the Surrey team, to ask me what was happening. When I told them, they assured me that the woman was indeed an authentic and reliable hypnotist of their acquaintance. On hearing that, I did not hang up as I might well have done.

Instead, I agreed to be hynotized over the telephone, standing there in the England dressing-room in the middle of a Test match and padded up ready to go in. At the time it seemed that I could hardly feel any worse. My jaw was aching, I could hardly speak, I was still feeling the after-effects of my illness and I thought that, if nothing else, this might cheer me up.

Besides, the idea of being told – even by an unknown woman hypnotist – that I would score many more runs appealed to me! 'Are you ready?' she asked. 'I want you to choose a spot on the wall and concentrate on it.' As there was a calendar featuring a naked girl hanging on the wall immediately in front of me I did not find this difficult.

I will not reveal here what part of her anatomy I focused on, but I concentrated as instructed while the voice on the phone repeated over and over again the things she had said before, her voice apparently becoming softer and softer and my eyes becoming heavier and heavier.

Eventually she said: 'You are now completely hypnotized and your eyes are closed. Are they closed?'

'Yes, they are.'

'You are completely under my spell and you will feel no ill-effects when you come round. Now your legs are beginning to feel heavy. Try to pick your left leg up.'

I tried but could not. She then asked me to pick up my right leg and I could not move that, either. Then she went on:

'Now the pain is going from your cheek, now you can open your mouth. Open it wide.'

I obeyed her instructions, though all the time I was vaguely aware of what was happening on the field. Suddenly a wicket fell. Arnold was in next with only Willis before me and some of the team began to hammer on the window of the phone booth.

All I wanted to do was stay there and listen to this unknown woman tell me what a great player I was! Then I heard one of the England team say: 'Christ – he's hypnotized', and finally the woman said she would snap her fingers and I would come out of the trance.

As she snapped her fingers, I opened my eyes. She asked if I was feeling all right, thanked me for being a good subject and hung up before I could ask her name. To this day I do not know who she was.

I am not sure how deeply I went into that hypnotic trance, but I certainly felt less pain afterwards. The only trouble was that her prophecy about many more runs was not immediately fulfilled because I made only another five before I was last man out with England totalling 545.

But I must have made history as the only England player to be hypnotized, not only during a Test match but in the middle of an innings, though many of my friends stare at me curiously when I tell them this story.

I have never heard from my lady hypnotist since that remarkable day, but if she reads this I would like to thank her for her efforts on my behalf. I did not realize it at the time but I was about to go on a tour where the presence of a hypnotist to soothe the nerves would have been most welcome. . . .

9

Enter Thomson and Lillee

Who started the bouncers? – unorthodox methods pay off for Greig – the most frightening bowling I have ever seen – why I did not blame Thomson – we lose a Test and I break a thumb – Cowdrey answers the call

To tour Australia is the ambition of every English cricketer. I am no exception and I was feeling on top of the world when we flew out in October 1974. The mood of the party was good, too. We knew it would be a hard series – they always are – but we thought we were equipped to do a good job.

What we did not know, indeed what no one suspected then, was that we were in for a battering from two fast bowlers called Dennis Lillee and Jeff Thomson. They were the main reason for Australia's comprehensive victory.

Looking back now, I can appreciate that almost anything that could go wrong for us on that tour did so, starting with Mike Denness's illness and continuing with one injury after another to various players. Yet up to the first Test we did better than most MCC teams in the state matches, winning two and having the better of two draws, and all the time we saw little from Australia's Test players to make us worried.

Maybe this was a classic example of players building themselves up for the big occasion or perhaps it was just lack of match practice, but batsmen like Redpath and Walters, for instance, gave no indication of the problems they were to cause.

More to the point, at that stage I had a close look at Lillee, Thomson and Walker and came firmly to the conclusion that

Walker was the man to watch. Encountering him for the first time on a slow pitch in Melbourne, I respected the way he found an accurate length and line, extracted a little movement and cleverly changed his pace.

I had already taken the opportunity of scrutinizing Lillee during our first week in Australia when, very conveniently, he was continuing his come-back to full fitness in a state game against South Australia. After watching from all angles I felt he did not have the pace to be as devastating as he was in 1972. I thought he would pick up occasional wickets, no more.

My introduction to Thomson was, in a cricketing sense, very brusque. He bowled the first ball of our game against Queensland and it lifted off a length and whacked me painfully in the throat. I still wince when I think about it.

That seemed to set the pattern for the Test series. We were always ducking and weaving and not always successfully. Even then, just to complete my trio of disastrous private forecasts, I did not think Thomson would be in Australia's Test team.

Quick he most certainly was, but most of us felt his pace had been exaggerated by the uneven bounce of the Brisbane pitch. And he was wildly inaccurate, with an alarming tendency to spray the ball all over the place. Too raw for Test cricket, we thought, and our theories were strengthened when he took only two wickets in the Queensland match (both mine).

In that game Greg Chappell played exceptionally well to make a century and a fifty. He was clearly going to be a problem to our bowlers, I felt, so at least I made one successful forecast!

We were in pretty good heart as the first Test approached, although we still had our problems. Mike Denness had been in and out of hospital for blood tests, but he was fit to play, although obviously short of match practice.

Bob Willis was suffering from jarred kneecaps which were to plague him throughout the series and David Lloyd chipped a finger during fielding practice. This meant that Brian Luckhurst partnered me, but before the game started our main worries concerned the Woolloongabba pitch.

There had been heavy rain before we arrived in Queensland, which was the only excuse for the poor pitch that had been provided for the preceding state match. In view of everything, not least a series of behind-the-scenes squabbles concerning the ground staff, we did not see how the Test pitch would be any better and we were right.

It was a pity for the Gabba, which once lagged behind Australia's major grounds, is now a beautiful setting for a Test match, with its new stands and ample facilities, but unfortunately – at least while we were there – without a pitch to compare with them.

It was at Brisbane, too, that we noticed the trend to leave more grass on the pitches. Apparently four years earlier, when Australia had no one to counter Snow, Willis and Lever, the pitches had been closely cut. Now, as Lillee and Thomson emerged as the men of the series, we found pitches everywhere well grassed, even Adelaide and Melbourne which are not normally happy hunting grounds for fast bowlers.

Under the circumstances we expected Ian Chappell to put us in when he won the toss at Brisbane, but he batted and at stumps on the first day Australia were 219 for six. Obviously that suited us. Several batsmen got out trying to hook, but I would not say we over-indulged in bouncers on that opening day.

The next morning we certainly did. Even Lillee was caught off his gloves, falling inelegantly to the ground as he tried to hook Greig. This was the start of a personal, private contest between this pair which they kept up throughout the series.

The atmosphere was always electric whenever one was bowling to the other and with their antics they provided many moments of 'needle' which were rich entertainment for the huge crowds everywhere. Like most members of both teams, however, they were the best of friends off the field.

Australia recovered well to reach 309, rather more than they should have made, but by Test-match reckoning a total that was only just adequate. Then came the first taste of Thomson and Lillee for Luckhurst and myself – and I soon realized I had underestimated Lillee.

His first over was faster than anything he had produced in Adelaide and he also managed to make the ball leave the bat and bounce a lot. Thinking of my 'pair' in my only previous Test appearance against Australia, I was glad to get off the mark with an edged four, and then as Thomson started to steam in from the other end we realized for the first time how difficult batting was going to be.

E

Luckhurst and I had a conference in mid-pitch and decided the only practical approach was not to play at anything we did not have to, in the hope that the bowlers would tire, but we did not have much chance to put that theory to the test because soon afterwards Luckhurst was brilliantly caught down the legside by Marsh.

This was another example of Thomson's ability to make the ball lift regularly from just short of a length. With most bowlers, Luckhurst would have been aiming a stroke through mid-wicket to that delivery; with Thomson's pace he found it impossible to take evasive action and was caught off his glove.

The uneven nature of the pitch, plus the real pace of this pair, meant that we were soon hopping about, uncertain about what the ball would do next, apprehensive about committing ourselves to strokes, and we were deep in trouble as Fletcher, Denness and myself were all dismissed.

Edrich, however, played a brave innings, taking blows on the elbow, hand and body while Greig launched himself into a characteristically impudent one which started when he greeted Lillee with a polite 'Good morning, Dennis' when he arrived in the middle. The fast bowler replied: 'Get up there – now it's your turn!'

Greig motivates himself by provoking other people and now he rode his luck in superb style, standing up to hit the ball rather than prod uncertainly at it, and he played a series of marvellous strokes through the covers, hitting the ball on the rise every time.

At times he was unorthodox, notably when he slashed short-pitched deliveries high over the slips, but it was a formula which paid off in circumstances where it was no good waiting for the bad ball to hit. On that pitch, with those bowlers, there was no such thing as a bad ball.

All the time Greig did his best to upset Lillee with his theatrical antics. Once he pretended to head a bouncer away and when he drove him through the covers for four with a really high-class stroke he shouted, 'Take that, Lillee!' and signalled the runs himself for good measure.

Greig was obviously enjoying every minute of it, but the rest of us had mixed feelings at the sight of an obviously hostile fast bowler being aroused to a frenzied pitch like this. After all, there were still five Test matches to come!

Eventually, Greig completed his century – a remarkable one – and then perished as he had succeeded, driving at a wide one. Later in that innings the pattern was set for the indiscriminate use of bouncers when Underwood, Lever and Willis were all hit. There could have been a serious injury, but, as on the previous day when our own bowlers were doing it, the umpires, Tom Brooks and Robin Bailhache, let it pass.

But that was nothing compared with the fast bowling that greeted Luckhurst and myself on the fourth evening after Australia had declared setting us to make 335 to win. Marsh and Walters had taken our attack apart when we thought we could contain them, helped, I think, by the inability of Lever and Willis to fire at full pace because of injury.

We were left with an awkward last hour in which I faced the most frightening fast bowling I have ever seen. Thomson and Lillee ran like madmen. They were not bowling bouncers but deliveries which lifted unpredictably from just short of a length.

Three of them whistled by my chin and because the light was poor one of the umpires warned Thomson to pitch the ball up. Thomson clearly was not having any. The next four balls whistled past my face and off we went.

I certainly did not blame Thomson. After all, he was not bowling deliberately short of a length, merely making the most of his own pace and the uneven pitch. Because of the conditions he was hardly going to bowl me a few half-volleys, nor did I expect any.

Now it was a question of whether we could survive the last day, for we had no hope of making such a substantial total. At first we felt the game could be saved, but our optimism was misguided and we were in all kinds of trouble against Thomson and Lillee.

Edrich had a pain-killing injection in his hand but did not stay long. I hung on for ninety-five minutes before being caught at slip, but Denness, Fletcher and Greig were out in successive overs and it was obvious that there was no way we could survive.

There was another flurry of bouncers at the lower-order batsmen and we were not only beaten but cruelly hit by injuries. After a sleepless night I discovered that my right thumb, which had been struck by deliveries from both Thomson and Lillee, was broken and would keep me out of action for at least a fortnight.

The injuries to Edrich and Lloyd had already prompted the tour selection committee to ask for Colin Cowdrey to be flown out at once. In the dressing-room this naturally aroused much discussion. No one quibbled about the choice of Cowdrey, but when we got around to discussing other candidates the most popular name was that of Basil D'Oliveira and he was forty-three – at least – at that time.

No one expected Cowdrey to be plunged into action immediately, but he had to play in the second Test at Perth within five days of arriving when it was learned that Edrich had broken a bone in his hand.

On top of everything else we played badly in the match before the Test and were well beaten by Western Australia. Our position was so grim that poor Brian Luckhurst, whose form had completely deserted him, had to play in the Test match when it would have been kinder to leave him out. All we could hope for, barring miracles, was to try to draw this match and in doing so buy time for the third Test at Melbourne when we would, hopefully, be back to full strength.

Meanwhile, the spirits of many members of the MCC party were given a lift by the arrival of their wives – my wife Jill among them – though naturally we would have preferred them to come into a more relaxed and successful atmosphere.

10

Wives on Tour – and why not?

Thomson and Lillee wreck our theory – what the curator said about Headingley – Walters flays us and we lose again – an exchange of words with Lillee – I miss a Test century and a world record – did the Australians lose their nerve?

The subject of cricketers' wives joining them on tour has always, apparently, been a contentious one. In our case they were immediately a target for certain critics, particularly as the Test and County Cricket Board had instructed that they could stay in the same hotels as the players for only twenty-one days.

As most of them had travelled under regulations that meant they had to be in Australia for a minimum of six weeks, there were obvious difficulties. We solved them by finding private accommodation, but as many people were only too ready to blame the presence of our wives for indifferent performances in Test matches and for various imaginary troubles between members of the touring party, I think it is time a player's point of view was heard.

These days we play so much all-the-year-round cricket and do so much travelling that I believe players become more conscious of the strain on their family life. Some players go for years without a break from the game.

The Australian tour, for instance, was the third successive winter away from home for many of us. On top of that, the structure of county cricket in the seventies means that even when we are playing in our own country we spend a lot more time travelling and in hotels than in the old days.

Under the circumstances it is surely understandable that the majority of players prefer to have the company of their wives on tour whenever possible, provided they are able to pay for them and that permission is granted by Lord's.

This is, after all, supposed to be an enlightened era. I know women are still barred from certain sacrosanct cricket pavilions up and down the country, but personally I like having my wife around. I want her to share some of the wonderful way of life that cricket has given to me.

As for my form, she does not affect it – except for the better! And in Australia there were a number of players, including Mike Denness, Keith Fletcher and Geoff Arnold, whose form improved noticeably after their wives had joined them.

I hope our cricket authorities will continue to take a tolerant view of wives on tour because there is, I believe, a very real danger that some players would turn down a tour if their wives were unable to join them. Indeed, there were some who would have thought twice about going to Australia.

I dare say a few eyebrows will be raised at that, but since the war cricket has had to learn to adopt a modern outlook in many respects and as far as I am concerned that means there should always be a place for wives, briefly, on any major cricket tour.

Wives or no wives, we were again well beaten in the second Test. This match quickly exploded our theory that we might handle Thomson and Lillee more comfortably on a pitch that was more trustworthy than Brisbane's. This one was a beauty to bat on, but we failed to make the most of it and it said much about our poor performance that Cowdrey, who had managed to squeeze in only a few hours at the nets after flying in, did as well as anyone and set a fine example of how to get in line against fast bowling.

The pitch itself was not as fast as we thought it might be, though Thomson and Lillee certainly were. The day before the Test started we all went to make our usual inspection of the all-important strip, but we could not distinguish it from the rest of the square because it was so green.

When we asked the curator if he was planning to take some of the grass off, he said with a wry smile: 'Well, we haven't forgotten Headingley in 1972!' a reference to the spinner's pitch which helped England to square that series.

At Perth Australia's catching was brilliant. On the first

day of the Test they held eight catches that I considered to be world-class and because of this they punished us for every mistake we made. This was another difference between the teams here; while our batsmen seemed to edge everything, theirs enjoyed a lot of playing and missing and we never made the breakthrough we needed.

Doug Walters flayed our attack to make a brilliant century in one session and we were beaten in four days. Once again we found it impossible to combat a non-stop bombardment of pace from both ends.

As we prepared for the third Test at Melbourne, where I was able to return, it was clear that our batting was still demoralized from our initial pounding in Brisbane. I could not help wondering if things would have been different if the series had started on a pitch which gave a fairer balance between bat and ball.

At the same time it was clear that in Thomson and Lillee Australia had found a phenomenal fast-bowling combination, not least in their ability to keep coming back, apparently more hostile than ever. Thomson, particularly, would regularly return after an ordinary-looking opening spell and pick up two or three cheap wickets when the ball had lost its shine. In fact, he preferred the old ball because he could control it more.

Even though the Melbourne pitch was slow (we were not surprised to find it was grassier than earlier in the tour), Thomson and Lillee were still dangerous. Indeed, we now appreciated that they were going to be a problem on any kind of pitch.

Even so, there was much about our peformance in this Test that was heartening. In the end we were rather lucky to escape with a draw, but at this stage we still felt the series could be saved, although by now the tour, from our point of view, was developing into a series of ifs and buts.

What would have happened if Mike Hendrick had not gone off injured after bowling only two overs? If Bob Willis had had someone to support him as he bowled superbly to take five for sixty-one, his best Test figures? Or if Fred Titmus had achieved some of the lbw decisions he gets in England to a ball pitching on middle and leg and drifting towards the off stump?

From my point of view I will remember this Test for my highest innings of the series. There were far too few impressive ones for my satisfaction and I seemed destined to receive a murderously unplayable delivery time and time again.

That happened here, too, but at last in the second innings, as David Lloyd and I put on 115 for the first wicket, I felt the pleasure of the ball flowing off the middle of the bat for the first time for weeks. You must wonder why we managed to conquer Thomson and Lillee then, yet failed so often in the other Tests.

I think it was a combination of factors, not least a pitch which was slow and low, which meant that we were not in too much trouble against short-pitched bowling. Indeed, we were able to cut and hook which forced Thomson and Lillee into overpitching for the only time in the series.

We enjoyed it rather more than they did, for once, and at one stage Lillee was spoken to by an umpire for swearing at me. This happened after I had steered him, not quite intentionally, wide of third slip to the boundary.

With a few runs under my belt I was not at all worried by Lillee's impressive vocabulary, but there was a slight hold-up while Ian Chappell was acquainted with the situation by the umpire.

Ironically, after all that, I got out to Ashley Mallett and thus missed my first Test hundred against Australia by ten runs and finished just short of Bobby Simpson's world record of 1381 Test runs in a calendar year. Since 2 February, I had scored 1379 in twenty-two innings, hitting five centuries.

I would have achieved both feats if I had carried on playing strokes, but there was a sudden rush of wickets and I felt it to be the best interests of the team to close up one end while we rebuilt. I was wrong, became bogged down and got myself out with a poor shot.

But we had done enough to ensure a remarkable and dramatic last day, which began with Australia needing 242 to win with all their wickets standing. Frankly, I thought we had not made enough runs, but we broke through early on rather remarkably with three lbw decisions and after that the game tilted first one way and then the other, with Greig using the new ball in place of Hendrick and Titmus able to bowl after all, despite a painful blow on the knee which had threatened to reduce us to three bowlers.

When the last hour (which means a minimum of fifteen

overs in Australia) began they needed fifty-four with four wickets left. It was the perfect finish to a Test that had been watched by more than a quarter of a million spectators, but I thought Australia lost their nerve in the final session, which was strange for a team two up in the series.

Our bowlers, especially Greig and Underwood kept things tight, but Marsh, particularly, surprised me by playing a very subdued innings at a time when two or three singles an over were all that Australia needed to win and go three up in the series with three Tests remaining. They were there for the taking because the field was pushed back.

This seemed to suggest that Australia were not so bold and dashing when there was an element of risk involved, but we did not dwell too much on the whys and wherefores of the situation. We were highly relieved not to be three down and in the belief that our spinners might be effective on the slower pitches of Adelaide and Melbourne, again, we still felt the series could be saved.

I I

Denness drops out . . .

Captaincy is like managing a football club – Denness studies himself on television – why we tried to change our methods – more bouncers and a surprise move by the umpires – protective 'armour' for English batsmen – why Lillee thought he was lucky – Edrich's courage cannot save the Ashes

The drama in Sydney started before a ball was bowled in the fourth Test when Mike Denness decided to stand down from the England team and to hand over the captaincy to John Edrich. Most of the Press, both English and Australian, had been calling for this – even after only two Tests! – but when it actually happened it was still something of a bombshell, particularly as Mike broke the news to the rest of the team less than twenty-four hours before the match.

Personally, I felt he showed courage and character in doing what he did. It was something, we were told, that had never happened before on an MCC tour; or at least it was the first time a captain had dropped out and *admitted* it was because of his poor form.

By his action, Denness got the tour selection committee out of an awkward predicament. We were two down in the series and under pressure to do something about our batting. The arrival of Cowdrey meant that when everyone was fit we had an extra batsman.

Someone had to go. In Melbourne it had been Keith Fletcher but now he returned and Mike Denness's decision led to all kinds of speculation about his future.

I do not envy any captain his job these days, whether he

leads England or a county team. It is a tough one and it has become increasingly like that of a football club manager: if you are not immediately successful, the cry goes up for a replacement.

Mike Denness had it tougher than most in Australia. His illness at the start of the tour left him looking tired and drawn, despite spending long hours confined to bed. But he never once complained. He was always approachable and sociable, too, though one subject I have never found easy to discuss with him is cricket.

Bearing in mind the pressure of a first Australian tour, the fact that we were losing heavily in the Tests as well as being battered by Thomson and Lillee, plus his personal battle to establish himself as captain and as a batsman, it was not surprising that Mike Denness struggled.

It was just too much for one human being to take, particularly one who never attempted to conceal that he was still learning the art of captaincy. This can take much longer than many people imagine.

I recall a certain county captain (not one that I played under, by the way!) of a few years ago. For the first two or three seasons his team never stopped moaning about him. In the end he became respected by them as a fine captain and tactician, a great leader and motivator of men, and his county had their fair share of success too.

The point I am making about Denness is that he was plunged in at the deep end when he took MCC to the West Indies, but gradually he showed that as well as putting his own ideas into practice he was prepared to accept sound advice from other, more experienced members of the team.

All captains can frequently benefit from a second opinion and most of them do not hesitate to ask. All right, some, like Brian Close and Ray Illingworth, need it less than most, but then they have been around a long time.

But now it was Denness's batting that was causing concern. His technique came in for some harsh criticism in the Press and on television and I must say there were some people who regarded it as the worst in the England team.

Even Denness himself did not appreciate that he was taking an initial step backwards with his right foot until it was pointed out to him. He then lost no time in analysing his technique by studying television film of himself in action.

Now I have always believed, possibly because of my own early struggles in the England team, that it is unfair to assess a batsman until he has had time to establish himself and I did not feel that Denness's approach was entirely wrong. After all, the circumstances of that series were unusual for most of us. For the first time in our cricketing careers we were faced with searing pace at both ends. We had to try to work out a way to combat it.

Getting into line was obviously technically correct, but we soon learned that no matter how much we employed orthodox methods to defend ourselves and our wickets, it was only a matter of time before we received an unplayable ball and got out, usually with very few runs to our names. No, we had to find methods not only to survive against Thomson and Lillee but to counter-attack them, and the steep bounce they were able to extract from Australian pitches.

The old theory about waiting for the bad ball did not always work, either. At their pace Thomson and Lillee bowled precious few deliveries that you could put away with any certainty. The one exception was that morning at Melbourne when, for the only time in the series, neither of them bowled particularly well.

So I felt that Denness was trying to work on similar lines to Greig, Knott and, sometimes, Fletcher, who had all experimented by slashing the ball hard over the slips. Indeed, after the first Test Denness discussed this stroke with Fletcher and I feel sure he came to the conclusion that it was one of the few ways to make runs against this pair.

Greig, of course, had used this stroke effectively when he made his century in Brisbane. He had also stood up and hit through the line, but that is a stroke that does not come easily to batsmen brought up on English pitches, and Greig had developed it in South Africa.

I am not saying that overnight English batsmen should try to change techniques which have stood the test of time, but emphasizing that in this series drastic measures were called for. We did not see how orthodox methods were going to succeed against the fastest pair of bowlers most of us had ever seen.

(On returning from Australia, by the way, I discussed this at length with my Warwickshire colleague Rohan Kanhai. He recalled the occasion when Bobby Simpson made a double century against Wes Hall and Charlie Griffith and, according to Rohan, continually backed away to give himself room to play strokes. I do not recall ever reading any fierce criticism of Simpson because of these methods.)

Although Denness was absent, things were otherwise much the same in the fourth Test. It is now history that we lost by 171 runs and surrendered the Ashes, and on the very ground where we had regained them four years earlier, too.

In some ways it was the most eventful, turbulent match of the series, played in a tremendous atmosphere. The crowds were said to be the biggest at Sydney since the bodyline series in 1932–3. Some of the action must have been similar, too.

Once again, we might have made more of an impression with only one fast bowler to deal with. Faced with two, our batting was undermined once more and this on what was basically a good batting pitch. Certainly, our bowlers could make little impression on it, but as it quickened up when it lost its first-day dampness it was ideal for Thomson and Lillee. The bounce was sometimes inconsistent, too, which made them more awkward.

Australia made 405, a very adequate total in view of our form with the bat and their bowling strength. There was another example of Lillee's explosive temper, this time when he was batting and was struck on the hand by a short-pitched ball from Greig.

This surprised nobody, because our own tail-enders had been subjected to so much short-pitched bowling throughout the series that some sort of retaliation seemed inevitable. When it happened Lillee dropped his bat and let loose a shower of expletives. Fletcher retrieved it for him, then hastily flung it down as Lillee turned his wrath on him. It may appear that Fletcher was harshly treated for his gentlemanly behaviour, but as he handed Lillee his bat he said: 'Now you know what it's like to have a dose of your own medicine.'

This incident brought a curious reaction from umpires Brooks and Bailhache, who officiated throughout the series. They warned Greig, which was understandable, but they then tried to legislate on the number of short-pitched deliveries that could be bowled at lower-order batsmen.

The confusion which resulted was perhaps typical of the

inconsistent attitude to this type of bowling which exists throughout the world today.

In the West Indies, for example, there appeared to be little or no concern about the proliferation of bouncers. In Australia, as far as I could see, at no time were umpires instructed to interpret strictly the existing law concerning intimidation, which in my view would have outlawed much of the bowling – from both sides – in this series.

Different countries, different attitudes from both players and administrators. I imagine you would hear a totally different point of view in India or New Zealand, two countries who have seen Test cricketers close to death as a result of short-pitched bowling.

Australia, of course, had a more sensitive attitude to short-pitched bowling during the infamous 'bodyline' series, and I noticed some of their players suddenly awoke to the dangers of it during their series against the West Indies last winter.

It is a complex problem because what may seem intimidatory bowling one day may look innocuous the next, depending on the bowlers, the batsman and the conditions. But as I have written elsewhere, it is up to the world's cricketing legislators to act strongly, to spell out, if necessary, what is and what is not permitted and to instruct umpires to take firm action whenever it is called for – before somebody *is* killed.

Meanwhile, despite the worthy intentions of the umpires, both Mallett and Thomson were later struck by short-pitched deliveries in that innings at Sydney, though the bowlers were not necessarily contravening the limit of bouncers previously imposed.

After all that we knew what to expect when we batted and by then some of us had followed the example of Colin Cowdrey and were wearing a protective 'armour' of foam rubber across our chests and down the left side of the rib cage (in the case of right-handed batsmen). These were made to measure by Bernard Thomas, our physiotherapist, and were held in position round the neck by elastic.

Sure enough, the first ball of our innings, from Lillee, was a bouncer of massive proportions. I ducked and watched it soar over my head and then, still rising, comfortably clear Rodney Marsh and go on for four byes like something launched into outer space.

As I straightened up, the elastic of my chest protector snapped and wrapped itself round my neck. For a moment I had the impression that I was being slowly strangled.

Since I had enough problems with Thomson and Lillee anyway, I discarded my foam rubber for good, just in time to encounter a spell of bowling from Lillee that was as fast as any I have ever faced, though not as terrifying as at Brisbane. Ironically, or perhaps because of this, it was Walker who got me out.

We made 295, which would have been a lot less if the Australians' catching had matched their brilliance at Perth. In the second innings, unable to set any attacking fields because we were so far behind, we were outplayed, with Redpath scoring a solid century and Greg Chappell a marvellously fluent one.

Though we were deep in trouble, we entertained the Australians, as usual, to a drink in our dressing-room that night. This was always the privilege of the fielding side and I think it is worth stressing that no matter what went on in the middle during that series it was forgotten at close of play.

Most players on both sides were happy to have a quiet drink and a chat to the opposition. From my point of view it gave me the opportunity to get to know Thomson and Lillee and explore their personalities rather more than I cared to out in the middle.

Thomson, I discovered, was a very quiet fellow, reluctant to talk about himself and his achievements. He did not have the swagger of some fast bowlers of my acquaintance and he gave me the impression that his notorious, much-quoted interview about wanting to hit batsmen and see blood on the pitch was something of an exaggeration.

Lillee, so quick to flare up in the middle, was pleasant, easy-going and sociable off the field, but he would not discuss his own bowling – possibly to avoid giving away trade secrets – until the series was over. Then he surprised me by admitting that he considered himself lucky to have got past the first Test because of his injured back. He said that before the series started he thought he would never again be able to bowl genuinely fast and added: 'When I was bowling medium pace in the state matches it wasn't for your benefit – it was because I just couldn't bowl any faster.'

But that was after it was all over. As we began our second

innings at Sydney, needing 400 to win – or, more to the point, to bat seven hours for a draw – Lillee launched himself with a series of bouncers at me and was warned again for overdoing it.

Curiously enough, although I made only thirty-seven, I considered this innings to be as good as any I had ever played, bearing in mind the quality of the fast bowling and the pitch, which was probably the fastest of the series.

Unfortunately for the needs of the team, my stay was all too short. Once again we were bowled out in less than a day, despite the bravery of Edrich who returned to battle it out after ducking into a ball from Lillee which did not bounce and which cracked a rib (he was not wearing one of Bernard Thomas's protectors).

Keith Fletcher was involved in another mishap which illustrated the sheer pace and menace of the Australian attack. He was struck by a ball from Thomson which deflected fractionally from his glove on to his head, from where it rebounded towards cover point . . . and was almost caught by Ross Edwards as he flung himself full length.

Luckily Keith was wearing his cap and the dressing-room joke was that he had been saved by St George and the dragon (the England badge). But the episode might well have been much more serious and it was hardly surprising that Keith did not survive that over.

The rest of our batting was not worthy of Edrich's courageous effort. After returning from hospital to continue his innings he was left high and dry. Tony Greig, so often the hero, was a villain this time, getting himself stumped after batting some three hours.

The fact that only five overs remained when we were eventually beaten, thanks to some stubborn defending by Willis and Arnold, showed that the game could have been saved. The Ashes had gone and our dressing-room was a gloomy place that evening.

By now we were all so jaded, mentally and physically, that we would have given anything for a break. I believe we would have felt that way regardless of the way the series was going. The trouble was that our tour itinerary was so tight that we had scarcely had a day off. We had spent most of our rest days practising because of our poor form, so we had hardly helped our own cause.

12

. . . and fights back

We waste our big chance – the mystery of Titmus and a spinner's pitch – I bag another 'pair' – a glimpse of how it might have been – Lillee's psychological hold over me – a Test victory at last – a memorable series but was it all cricket?

Tasmania would have provided the ideal opportunity to wind down if we could have played just one game and not two against the same team. One of the pitches, at Launceston, was so bad we had to warn our fast bowlers to cut down their run-ups. The irony of that, after what had been happening in the Tests, was not lost upon us.

One man who benefited from both games, however, was Mike Denness. His six-hour, unbeaten 157 on that untrust-worthy pitch was the work of a very determined man and he regarded himself as ready to return for the fifth Test, which was as well because by now John Edrich had learned that his cracked rib would keep him out.

You may wonder what our approach to this Test match was with the series – and the Ashes – already lost. Quite honestly, we felt the need to try to regain some of our pride by proving we could do better and by winning the last two Tests if possible.

But things went dreadfully wrong at Adelaide. Rain washed out the first day and high winds also blew off the covers in the middle of the night, much to the consternation of the local authorities who had taken the trouble to have the square specially 'guarded'.

F

As a result the pitch was still wet when Denness won the toss on the second morning and with both Derek Underwood and Fred Titmus in the team, and the prospect of the pitch drying under the hot sun, there was no hesitation about putting Australia in.

Eventually, as expected, the ball began to turn and lift. Australia lost their first five wickets for eighty-four runs, all to Underwood, who went on to take the first seven. Yet while this was happening Titmus bowled only one over in which, significantly, he got one ball to turn and lift so extravagantly that it went over Doug Walters' left shoulder from outside the off stump.

Why Titmus did not bowl again while the pitch was at its most helpful is something I found hard to understand.

Obviously Mike Denness thought the best approach was to use Underwood at one end and let the quicker bowlers keep things tight at the other. To a certain extent this plan was upset because Greig, bowling his quicker stuff, did not have one of his better days.

We did not get Australia out until they had totalled 304, which was probably twice as many as they expected to make on that pitch.

By mid-afternoon the pitch had dried and was much easier, but we contributed to our problems by allowing Terry Jenner a generous amount of spin, which he plays better than pace, and his innings of seventy-four was the cornerstone of Australia's recovery.

We never regained our grip. It was almost as if the fates had decided that we had been given our big chance and had failed to make the most of it. I was the first to suffer. In Lillee's first over the next morning he beat me with a late outswinger and I collected my first nought of the series.

Apart from Denness and Fletcher, who each made their highest score of the series – fifty-one and forty respectively – our batting was poor and, losing our last six wickets for forty-two runs, we were all out for 172. It was the now familiar story – Thomson and Lillee! They were able to exploit slight indentations in the pitch which made the ball jump about and at their pace there was no time for our batsmen to adjust.

The rest day brought the news that Thomson had injured a

shoulder playing tennis and would take no further part in the match, but this was counter-balanced when Willis, still bothered by knee trouble, broke down in the nets and could not bowl in Australia's second innings.

Consequently, although Underwood took his haul of wickets in the match to eleven, Australia made 272 for five with the minimum of trouble and Ian Chappell's declaration invited us to make 405, or one more than Bradman's Australians had scored to win at Headingley in 1948. Assuming that Chappell was aware of it at the time, this showed a nice, sly sense of humour.

Not that we were in any mood to appreciate it. Once again it was a question of survival and for me it was all too brief. For the second time in the match I was out in Lillee's opening over, though this time I put my dismissal down to anxiety to get off the mark.

I thus collected my second 'pair' against Australia. And despite Thomson's absence we were beaten by 163 runs by mid-afternoon the next day, even though Knott hit a typically flamboyant unbeaten century during which he regularly slashed Lillee, and the new ball, high over the slips, with strokes that were unorthodox but intentional.

It was a heartening knock, but we had still been beaten in four days. Considering we had put Australia in, it was a dismal performance. I doubt whether it is possible for any touring team to feel more dejected than we were when we arrived at Melbourne for the sixth Test.

Nor were we encouraged by the sight of another well-grassed pitch, which also had a wet patch about the size of a man's hand. Some attempt had been made to camouflage this, but Denness spotted it, though as it happened Chappell won the toss which prevented any discussion about putting Australia in again.

Then on that day in Melbourne, after being battered and beaten throughout Australia, we at last had a glimpse of how things might have been as we bowled them out for 152, the lowest total of the series. Conditions were perfect for our fast bowlers, particularly Peter Lever, who swung the ball in the humid atmosphere.

For once everything went right. Edged strokes went to hand, instead of avoiding the field, and we held our catches. Now it was up to our batsmen, but, alas, nothing had changed for me.

Watching the Australians bat, I had decided that as the ball was not bouncing unduly, I would attempt to get on to the front foot as often as possible. So much for theories!

In Lillee's first over he made two balls lift from not much short of a length and then he had me lbw. It was my third successive nought in successive Test innings. They had all lasted less than one over and at that stage I confess Lillee had built up a massive psychological stranglehold over me.

Next day Lillee bowled only two more overs before limping off with an injured foot. For the first time in the series we had neither Thomson nor Lillee to contend with and it was the perfect opportunity to prove the theory, frequently expounded in our dressing-room, that they were the only difference between the two teams.

Our total of 529 was proof enough. Suddenly Australia looked very ordinary. Their out-cricket lacked its usual sharpness and discipline. They dropped catches. They were still trying hard, of course, but they lacked the inspiration of having two great fast bowlers at their beck and call.

Denness and Fletcher, with a century each, made the bulk of the runs and Greig savaged the attack with a brilliant exhibition of stroke play. After dominating the series Australia found themselves 377 behind and needing to bat just over two days to save the game.

This is an awful long time, no matter what the quality of the batting. Australia, however, must have thought they were well on the way to achieving their object when they were 274 for three at stumps the next day, when we were without Lever, who was a temporary influenza victim.

One of those wickets was highly controversial when Ian Chappell was adjudged to have glanced a ball from Greig into Knott's gloves. There was an exchange of words, but the incident achieved nothing.

We went on to win by an innings and four runs. Greg Chappell and Redpath were the batsmen we thought might deprive us. Redpath, indeed, batted for another six hours. Throughout the series he occupied the crease for something like a total of five days, a vital and largely unsung contribution to Australia's success.

Analysing this series since it ended, I have reflected that England suffered thirteen injuries to Australia's two, which clearly affected the balance of our team if not necessarily the outcome of the Tests. I have also wondered how great English players from other eras, players like Denis Compton, Peter May and Len Hutton, would have played Thomson and Lillee.

Lillee was said by many Australians to be faster than Ray Lindwall. On hearing this, I asked Sir Leonard Hutton, who was in Australia on business and was a frequent visitor to our dressing-room, if he ever played the hook shot against Lindwall.

He thought for a moment, then he said: 'I would move across and get into position for the hook, then the ball would whistle past my ear . . . no, I never played the hook against Lindwall!'

Despite my many failures, I found it a tremendous experience playing against Thomson and Lillee, but at the same time I had certain reservations about the game I was supposed to be playing. Very often it was not cricket, not when I had to spend so much time defending myself. Many a time I walked out to the middle in a Test match knowing it was virtually a waste of time carrying a bat. I knew it would be used not so much to make strokes as to fend the ball off my body.

Any batsman who plays Test cricket should be able to adapt to cope with fast bowling sooner or later. To a certain extent Greig and Knott worked out ways to succeed and others tried to follow their example, but I could never have copied their methods.

I decided to stick to a technique which was based on old-fashioned virtues and which, after all, had eventually proved correct enough to make me an England player. There were times, it is true, when one failure after another made me wonder, but I believe that throughout the series I was genuinely dismissed more often than I brought about my own downfall and that was due to the quality of the bowling.

Strangely enough, up to the time of my three successive noughts, I had started to feel that at last I was coming to terms with the demands of the tour, with Australian conditions and with their fast bowlers, but in the end my confidence simply disappeared.

It was a frustrating experience for all of us, but to my knowledge there was not one other current English batsman who at that time could have improved our performances, bearing in mind all the circumstances of that tour, to a degree that could have changed the overall result of the series.

13

A Matter of Life and Death

The man who 'died' at the wicket – Greig and a twist of fate – why Lever bowled short – my worst experience on a cricket field – Bernard Thomas to the rescue – is this the answer to intimidation? – the best pitch in England – how I would change county cricket

Nothing would have given greater pleasure to me and the rest of the MCC party in Australia in February 1975 than to be told to pack our bags and forget all about cricket. After five months of living out of suitcases, six Test matches and a battering from Messrs Thomson and Lillee, the game had temporarily lost its charm.

Instead, we flew across the Tasman Sea for a two-match series against New Zealand that most of us could have done without and an experience concerning a young man playing in his first Test match that none of us will ever forget. His name is Ewan Chatfield. If he never sets foot on an international cricket field again he will be remembered as the batsman who 'died' at the wicket and in doing so grimly reminded the rest of the cricket world of the risks we all take when we play this game.

The drama of that sunny morning at Auckland's Eden Park is still vividly etched on my mind. I can recall, too, the series of emotions – shock, anguish, sympathy, and finally, relief – that overtook me when Chatfield deflected a ball from Peter Lever on to his temple and collapsed at the crease.

And later, when we had established that Chatfield had recovered, we had time to reflect upon the irony of the situation. It had not, after all, happened in one of those tense, dramatic

Test matches in Australia with Thomson and Lillee pounding in, but on an almost deserted ground in New Zealand and at a time when a Test match was as good as won and lost.

Looking back, I think the simplicity and the very ordinariness of the occasion helped to emphasize the severity of what happened. There was nothing to distract our attention from the pathetic figure of Chatfield writhing and twitching on the ground.

The build-up to the Chatfield incident had been a pleasant Test match, played on a good cricket wicket, which England had dominated. The New Zealanders were confident of gaining their first-ever win against us – particularly after our problems in Australia – but we made a massive total, largely due to Keith Fletcher and Mike Denness, and they followed on.

The match might have ended on the fourth day – such is fate – when Tony Greig exploited a wearing pitch to take five wickets, but one or two close catches eluded us in the final session and Chatfield stayed with Surrey's Geoff Howarth until the close.

Another twist of fate concerned Greig's spinning finger, which was too sore for him to bowl on the final morning. Otherwise he would have bowled instead of Lever and an incident which made headlines throughout the world would not have happened.

The atmosphere that morning was certainly one of anti-climax. The match seemed as much of a foregone conclusion as any game of cricket can be and, as the previous day had been a rest day, at least one New Zealand reporter had checked out of his hotel and gone home, convinced that nothing much could happen and no doubt thinking he was doing his newspaper a favour by cutting down expenses.

We all felt much as he had done. There was just a handful of casually interested spectators, an atmosphere quieter than on the last day of a dying English county match, and for three-quarters of an hour or so Howarth and Chatfield survived without much difficulty.

Lever had bowled one or two shortish deliveries which Chatfield had played quite well. Then he tried a bouncer which struck Chatfield's glove; instead of carrying to one of the close fielders, however, it went straight down to the ground.

Let me say straightaway that I considered this to be quite

Edgbaston 1975, Mike Denness leads England for the last time. *Back left to right*: Keith Fletcher, Geoff Arnold, Tony Greig, Chris Old, Graham Gooch, Dennis Amiss. *Front:* Derek Underwood, John Snow, Mike Denness, John Edrich, Alan Knott.

A new captain and new faces in the England team, Lord's 1975. *Back left to right*: Bob Woolmer, Graham Gooch, Chris Old, Peter Lever, Dennis Amiss, David Steele, Barry Wood. *Front:* John Snow, Alan Knott, Tony Greig (captain), John Edrich, Derek Underwood.

Playing my favourite stroke, the cover drive.

On top for once. I square cut Lillee to the boundary in the third Test against Australia at Melbourne in December 1974. I just missed a century and a world record.

My running between the wickets has not always been flawless! Here, another near thing against Pakistan at the Oval in 1974 as I just beat Aftab Baloch's throw.

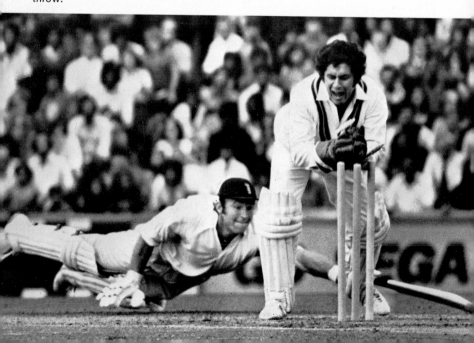

A man called Boycott.

Packing for my first tour of Australia, watched by my wife Jill with son Paul (*left*) and daughter Rebecca.

a legitimate ploy by Lever. I do not agree that tail-end batsmen should receive short-pitched deliveries the moment they come in, but Chatfield had been around for some time and Lever was entitled to dig one in to try to get some life out of a pitch that had nothing in it for a fast bowler.

Then it happened. Lever, obviously appreciating that Chatfield had looked uncomfortable against the first one, dug another one in short. It struck Chatfield's glove, as the bowler had intended, but as the batsman averted his head, it was deflected on to his left temple, with an awful crack that sounded like a rifle bullet.

The next few moments were the worst I have ever experienced on a cricket field. From my position close to the bat I watched horrified as Chatfield staggered around the crease, with his eyes flickering, before finally sinking to the ground.

Lever sank to his knees in tears and the rest of us crowded round Chatfield in a state of panic. It was clear at once that this was no ordinary accident. Someone raced to the pavilion for a doctor. The rest of us stood around, helpless, wanting to do something but hesitant and terrified in case we should make things worse.

As he lay there with his body convulsing, Chatfield's tongue became lodged in his throat and he started to choke. His face began to go blue and our distress increased as we realized that here was a fellow cricketer dying in our midst and we were apparently powerless to help him.

Still there was no sign of a doctor, but by now Bernard Thomas, the MCC physiotherapist, had sprinted out to the middle. He prised Chatfield's tongue from the back of his throat and held it while he administered mouth-to-mouth resuscitation – the kiss of life – and an ambulance man massaged his heart.

There was no sign of life. Suddenly I was reminded of the incident when Roger Davis, of Glamorgan, was struck on the head by my Warwickshire colleague Neal Abberley while fielding at short leg during a championship match. He, too, needed the kiss of life.

Now, as then, the sky seemed to grow dark, even at noon on a beautiful New Zealand day, and the faces of my England team mates were ashen with concern. Chatfield was carried off on a stretcher and as Mike Denness led a solemn England team behind it, I had the gruesome impression of marching in the cortège at a small private funeral, instead of being a member of a team which had just won a Test match.

Happily, Bernard Thomas's efforts had worked. Before we reached the pavilion Chatfield was able to make a feeble croaking noise. In the pavilion medical room he continued to recover with the help of oxygen, though in the confusion nobody had been able to locate it at first.

Eventually Chatfield was taken to hospital and even as he left the ground there was still no sign of a doctor. One should be in attendance at all games at first-class level and especially Test matches.

Bernard Thomas's prompt action was undoubtedly the only reason that Chatfield is alive today. It also prevented the need for what might well have been a bitter and embarrassing inquiry, yet even he might not have been there. He was suffering from mild food-poisoning and I remember his telling me that morning that he did not feel well enough to go to the ground. Like the rest of us, he probably felt it would be just a formality, but he went all the same, stressing it was his job to be there even if the game lasted only one ball more.

How wise he was! Throughout all this there was nothing we could do to console Lever, who was so distressed that for a time he seriously considered retiring from first-class cricket there and then. But the rest of the New Zealand team were quick to stress that they attached no blame to him and the whole episode ended more quickly and happily than anyone expected, with Chatfield recovered and out of hospital in time to watch the second Test at Christchurch, by which time Lever had overcome his misgivings and took part.

Inevitably, the incident provoked a good deal of discussion (including some profound comments by people who sat in judgement 13000 miles away in England) and in the England dressing-room there was – and still is – a great deal of concern about the amount of short-pitched bowling in the game today. There is certainly more of it nowadays than when I began my career. In those days bowlers seemed to regard it as a waste of time and energy bowling short at batsmen who did not play the hook and, therefore, were unlikely to get themselves out.

Why are there so many bouncers and other short-pitched deliveries today? One reason, I feel, is that pitches are more inconsistent in bounce than they were and consequently the short-pitched ball is a much more dangerous delivery if the batsman is uncertain about the height it is going to reach him.

I was delighted that the International Cricket Conference took the decision to outlaw the bouncer in last year's Prudential Cup by classing it as a no-ball. In one-day cricket that makes sense.

But while I would not want to deprive fast bowlers of a genuine attacking weapon in all other forms of the game, I trust that the unfortunate Chatfield incident will encourage cricket authorities everywhere to act strongly whenever there is an excess of short-pitched bowling, whether in a Test series or in a domestic competition.

If they do not, it is only a matter of time before a batsman – and I mean a batsman, not merely a tail-ender – is killed or suffers serious, permanent injury. There was even talk among some England players of wearing protective headgear after their experiences in Australia, but to me the one logical answer lies in firm umpiring.

Umpires are under more and more pressure these days, especially in Test matches and other important games where their split-second decisions can be analysed and queried by the television camera and the slow-motion action replay, but they have the power to warn bowlers who over indulge in short-pitched stuff. To me, it is a matter of common sense and discretion. No one wants to deprive the spectator of the thrill of seeing a hook for six off a bouncer – or the bowler of the right to try to unsettle the batsman with one – but when they are bowled all the time it is not good for the game.

Increased short-pitched bowling is just one aspect of the game today which concerns me. These days more and more bowlers rely on banging the ball into the pitch and trying to move it off the seam rather than swinging it through the air. This is because they have found these to be the most effective methods on the type of pitches we have been producing in England in the last few years. Even if the ball does not 'seam about' bowlers still dig it in short and I could name one or two who pitch it almost at their own feet to try to get it to lift.

They like to get batsmen on the back foot because in England most of them are very proficient at playing forward. It is, admittedly, very hard to dismiss competent front-foot players on our slow pitches, so bowlers try to make them apprehensive by dropping short. Even medium-pacers bowl just short of a length and when they do it to defensive fields the game becomes negative and dull.

What is the answer? It has been said before, but I will spell it out again. We need to cover our pitches to produce surfaces that are firm and true and with some pace and bounce. Then we will develop more genuine fast bowlers, stroke-playing batsmen, leg-spinners and finger-spinners who would have to learn how to flight the ball.

We would also outlaw – or at least show up for what he is worth – the phantom medium-pacer, trundling away just short of a length to defensive fields trying to exhaust the batsman's patience. Bowlers would have to learn to swing the ball again as their main hope of taking wickets.

Quicker pitches would also make life more difficult for the accumulator. You have all seen him, the batsman with limited ability and technique who is able to survive for hours on slow pitches and makes all his runs with nudges and deflections to the utter boredom of the spectator and frustration of the bowler.

It would be a cricketing Utopia, I know, but until it happens we will never develop batsmen who are confident enough to stand up and play off the back foot and hit through the line of the ball, knowing it will not deviate off the seam, as the best overseas players do.

How would we achieve this? I would not presume to tell groundsmen their job, but there is one place in England where, granted normal weather, you can always be certain of finding the ideal pitch – and if they can do it why not others?

If you have not already guessed, I am referring to the County Ground, Worcester, where at the start of a match the pitch has some pace and bounce and some movement while the ball is new. It then becomes a beautiful surface to bat on, rewarding the batsman who plays strokes or the bowler who has some pace; eventually, it starts to take spin so everybody in the game has a fair opportunity to display his skills.

Obviously the English climate will always interfere with pitch preparation, especially in the early part of the season. I feel, therefore, that we must allow for that and play county championship matches over four days and on covered pitches.

If groundsmen everywhere were to produce the best pitches

possible, knowing that they would be protected from rain, then I feel that a county championship consisting of sixteen four-day matches, with bonus points for batting and bowling, would be the fairest contest of all and would go some way towards putting our game on a par with the way they play it overseas.

It would take time to adjust, of course. You might have slow scoring and a few games drifting to stalemate at first, with several results depending on declarations, but gradually the positive players, the attacking batsmen, the fast bowlers and the quality spinners would come into their own.

To win the county championship a team would need to have the right blend of stroke-playing batsmen, bowlers of genuine pace and spinners who really spin, not just aim for the blockhole, and results would not depend so much on the luck of the toss, which in these days of uncovered pitches often decides who wins the match.

Teams would quickly catch on. If the 100-over limit on first innings were also abandoned, then the county championship would become a proper game of cricket once more and, as such, would provide a correct balance with the one-day game.

14

A Man called Boycott

*Opening pairs are like married couples – recriminations after a run out –
what we say to each other in the middle – how Boycott has helped me– his
'crime' against the Indians – a puzzling decision not to tour – a
batsman of skill and contradiction*

Geoffrey Boycott is to many people the enigma of modern
cricket, a player blessed with great ability, application and
determination, yet a man whose image tends at times to
appear rather complex. You cannot discuss cricket with anyone
anywhere in the world for long before his name crops up.

I first came across him during a second-team match at
Driffield when, like me, he was just another aspiring batsman.
Since then I have had the advantage of seeing him at close
range as his partner in many Test and international matches
for England, so these impressions of the man are sincere ones
acquired through sharing hours at the crease and in the
dressing-room with him.

An opening partnership, I have always felt, is like a marriage.
You have to work at it and there are good days and bad,
moments of triumph and tragedy, episodes of laughter and
despair. Geoffrey and I have experienced many of these
emotions together, though he did seem a bit aloof when we
first opened the England innings together.

That was against Australia in the Prudential Trophy at
Old Trafford in 1972. Mind you, in my early days in the
England team you were not exactly welcomed into the dressing-
room with open arms by everybody.

Some players seemed to resent a newcomer stepping into the

team, almost as if it meant the end of the road for an older player. These days it is different because most of the present England team came up together and they can all remember what it feels like to struggle to become established.

So perhaps I was not too surprised when I was not immediately accepted by Boycott. Maybe he thought, as I did, that Barry Wood ought to have been playing, having just made ninety against Lillee and company, particularly as this was his home ground. Still, the selectors preferred me and I found myself walking out to bat for the first time with a player I had always admired.

Walking, did I say? In our first few games together I almost had to jog to keep up with Geoff as he strode out to the middle. He left me in no doubt that he was the senior partner. He would always be one pace ahead of me and, of course, he always took strike. I remember wishing him 'Good luck' as cricketers invariably do to each other. He did not reply. It was only later, in the West Indies, that I learned that he did not approve of the term 'Good luck'. It was easy to understand why. To Boycott it suggested that he might need some good fortune to succeed.

He knew differently. He believed in ability. After that I changed it slightly to 'All the best', which seemed acceptable, but even then it was some time before we actually began talking to each other while we were batting together.

At first if I called for a run which he rejected he would give me a filthy look. And if I refused one of his calls he would look at me as if to say: 'Don't you know who's in charge out here?' Eventually he said he would do all the calling in that first partnership and I accepted because I think we both felt that I was only a temporary partner and we would not be seeing too much of each other.

As it happened, in that first match we ran pretty well together. It has not always been the case. Indeed, in our first Test match together against New Zealand at Trent Bridge the following year I ran Boycott out.

In the first innings we put on ninety-two, despite some uncertainty over one or two singles. Looking back, I think we were both very wary; I admit I am not the best runner or caller in the world and Geoff also had a reputation of being involved in a lot of run outs.

Mike Smith had always impressed upon me that there were enough ways of getting out, anyway, and I had it firmly in my mind that I was not going to be run out. After the first innings we agreed that we must call loud and clear – and then it happened. I drove Collinge through the vacant mid-off area. As I made the stroke, I shouted 'Two' and as we crossed I warned Geoff to have a look.

Turning, I saw Pollard about to pick the ball up and I noticed Geoff ground his bat and turn for a second run without looking. I realized that two runs were now out of the question because Pollard had fielded the ball so quickly, but Geoff may not have heard my warning to have a look, so as he turned I shouted 'No!' He said 'Yes, come on' and I replied 'No, no, no!'

As he kept coming, I turned and grounded my bat. I admit that in that situation the correct thing to do is to sacrifice your own wicket, especially if you are the junior partner as I was, but I was obsessed with not being run out. I turned my back on him and, as you can imagine, he said a few well-chosen words as he walked past.

Fortunately, I went on to make a century, which in a way justified my position. If I had struggled or let the run out affect me, I would have been criticized and rightly so. Later I learned that Geoff was so upset that he thought I had run him out on purpose. I did not think it was all my fault and imagined he would come and discuss the matter with me when he had cooled down.

He must have been waiting for me to do the same thing because we went through the rest of that match without speaking. This situation was something new to me, so I approached Ray Illingworth, the England captain, for advice. At his suggestion Boycott and I got together at the next pre-Test dinner where we patched it up and agreed, once more, that we must call loud and clear.

We naturally became more cautious after that, though there were no more run outs, just a few mix-ups. In the first Test against the West Indies at the Oval that year, for instance, I square cut Boyce for an easy two, turned for the second and saw to my dismay that Geoff was not running.

I was halfway down the pitch screaming at him to run before he set off and he just scraped home as Lloyd whistled the ball in over the stumps at his end. The explanaton was simple. He had not heard my original call because of the frenzied noise made by the large contingent of West Indians in the crowd.

At Edgbaston, in the same series, Geoff drove a ball to Kallicharran at mid-on and set off, but I sent him back. In his haste he collided with Murray, the wicketkeeper, and the pair of them went down in an undignified heap. I thought Geoff had been knocked out cold and he had still not moved when I walked down the pitch to see how he was.

As I leaned over him, his eyes slowly opened and he was startled to see my face peering anxiously down at him from just a few inches away. He said just two words – 'You — !' – and I found the situation so funny I could not stop laughing.

Gradually, though, we eliminated much of this uncertainty and in the West Indies that winter we began to blend together quite well, to help each other and we also started to appreciate each other's problems. In that series a sound opening stand was more important than ever and we developed the habit of talking to each other more between the overs.

Spectators, I know, often wonder what we talk about at such times. Usually it is a simple matter of saying something to build up your partner's confidence. He might, for instance, ask how you thought he coped with a certain awkward delivery and is reassured when you tell him he did well.

Sometimes you might be starting to become a little jittery, approaching a half-century or a hundred, or you might simply be taking too many risks. In every case it is the job of the other batsmen to give you a quiet warning or a reassuring word, whichever is needed.

These things are all part of an opening batsman's job and they are one reason why I have learned and benefited from batting with Geoff Boycott. Sometimes he has made it look so easy that his confidence has rubbed off on me. And, oddly enough, if you see him play and miss that can help, too. You think you cannot be doing too badly if the bowling is good enough to get past Boycott's bat.

With Boycott everything stems from the technique he has worked out for himself and his superb judgement of what to play and what to leave alone. Basically, his first movement is back and across to cover the off stump. This takes him right

G

in line behind the ball and, importantly, still leaves him sideways on so that he can take his bat away at the last moment if necessary.

He is always perfectly balanced, too, which means he can still play off the front foot when required and this he does with a big stride, thus avoiding the 'half-cock' stroke which can get you out, particularly if the ball is moving about, as it frequently is in English conditions.

When you add to this his unrivalled ability to concentrate, plus the Spartan way he looks after himself, shunning the social whirl and allowing himself no more than the occasional glass of beer, you can see how Boycott has become the formidable player he is.

He has never been one for late nights and he is clearly a loner, but I have often felt that if he were to possess a little more of the ability to relax away from the game, to have a laugh, a joke and a drink, it would help him, particularly when he strikes a bad patch, as we all do.

He has always impressed me as being very confident in his own ability and, like Ken Barrington, has developed a technique which eliminates risks and will always enable him to make runs regularly. He bats to make hundreds and when he was playing in Test cricket he knew, as we all know, the value of simply occupying the crease, even if you are not forcing the ball off the square.

In the last year or so his appetite for Test cricket has been questioned and no one knows whether he will ever play for England again. He dropped out of the home series against India in 1974 after his early failures and his decision not to tour Australia baffled and disappointed those of us who did make the trip.

Even so, I can readily sympathize with him. In the past few years, because of his reputation, Boycott has been the target of every cricketing country. He carried the burden of England's batting from the days when we had our share of high-class, experienced players into an era when we are still trying to find a settled side.

Opposing bowlers have known that if they dismissed Boycott cheaply they stood a fair chance of getting England out for a moderate score. Thus, fast bowlers the world over have not hesitated to let him have it and I honestly believe that in 1974 he came to the conclusion that he had had enough and needed a genuine break from cricket.*

You sometimes hear it levelled against him that he has become increasingly suspect against fast bowling. All I can say to that is that over the years he has a tremendous record which has been compiled against bowling of every kind.

None of us really likes fast bowling, anyway. Who enjoys being smashed in the ribs or on the arm or feeling the draught as the ball whistles past your head? And there have been famous players of the past, many of them household names, who were not renowned for playing it well.

In my book Boycott must compare with anyone, though I do feel that at the time of his withdrawal from the Test scene the bombardment had become too much for him. I also believe that at times Geoff has not reached the heights that he knows he is capable of scaling and when he falls short he feels guilty and disappointed and consequently becomes depressed.

There may also have been something not quite right about his technique in his last Test appearances, too. I think that even he did not know the answer to that and it may have had more to do with the mental strain of Test cricket than any actual flaw.

Looking back to his series of failures against the Indians in 1974, I do not think it was stressed enough at the time that Solkar, the man who kept getting him out, bowled exceptionally well, exploiting the conditions and making the ball move about. For an over or two, I think, he might have dismissed any batsman in the world.

His victim happened to be Geoff Boycott, who deep down inside must have regarded this as some sort of crime after facing all the world's great fast bowlers with a reasonable degree of success. Possibly he underestimated Solkar, and then became more and more depressed at getting out for one low score after another against an opening attack which he probably regarded as mediocre.

Since then, I have often wondered if it would have helped if Geoff had talked things over with either myself or other members of the England team. But you never like to pry into other people's problems unless invited and Geoff never sought

---

*These words were written before my struggles against Australia which you can read about in Chapter 15.

our assistance.* But I do know that if Geoff had come out with it and discussed his problems openly in the England dressing-room he would have received nothing but encouragement because he is such a fine player and everyone wanted to see him in the team – and scoring runs.

Having said that, I was saddened by his decision not to go to Australia and puzzled that he waited until the party had been announced before withdrawing. I dare say he had some worries over his benefit, which seems to affect the form of every player at some stage, but he had taken his break from Test cricket and it was unfortunate that a player of his calibre should turn down a tour of Australia, which, after all, is the one reason we all want to play for England.

Still, that is Geoffrey Boycott, a cricketer of rare skill and a character apparently full of contradictions. I confess that I find it hard to know the real Boycott, despite my experiences with him, and do not understand why he does the things he sometimes does.

Personally, I want to play for England, if I am considered good enough, as long as possible, regardless of failure or physical batterings. But in saying that I am mindful of the fact that I have not played at the highest level as long as Boycott. Nor have I achieved as much.

*It is interesting to see my own reaction to a similar situation in Chapter 15.

15

Out of the Test Team

Problems of a benefit year – Warwickshire finish empty-handed – another controversy at Headingley – my advice to Denness is not taken – Thomson and Lillee again – my doubts about Test cricket – Greig takes over the captaincy – David Steele's secret fear – the question I still have to answer

No English cricketer can have a greater test of his nerve, his skill and his physical and mental toughness than a tour of Australia. In my opinion it is the most demanding of all the tours we make and I have been on them all, except, of course, to South Africa who are currently in isolation.

When I returned from Australia and New Zealand before the start of the 1975 English season I knew I was jaded. I needed a break before the new season began, but David Brown, who had just taken over as Warwickshire's captain, requested that I train with everybody else and I respected his point of view.

But after five months of cricket and travelling I was hardly wild with enthusiasm about the endless rounds of lapping, circuit training, five-a-side football and basketball that Warwickshire indulge in before the start of each season and I must have cut a sorry figure as I lagged wearily behind everyone.

I also had something else on my mind – my benefit, which Warwickshire granted me that year. Nowadays, when it is increasingly difficult to play cricket and develop a career outside the game, a benefit is even more significant, even to someone like myself who has reached Test level and has travelled the world and been paid better than the average player.

The problem is how to prevent it affecting your form. Year after year you will see consistent, reliable county cricketers suffer lapses in their performances because they are concerned with their benefit activities. I was determined it was not going to happen to me.

It is important to have your benefit functions well organized and in that respect I was fortunate to be backed up by a committee efficiently run by Ken Purnell, a close friend, but even so it was still up to me to put in my fair share of work.

For instance, before the season began I found myself speaking at twenty different functions. In fact, I made the same speech so many times that one night six fellows, who must have heard it so often that they knew it backwards, stood up at the back of the room holding placards giving me marks out of ten!

I think that gives an indication of how much time a benefit takes up and why cricketers are affected. At a time when I should have been relaxing, preparing for a strenuous season ahead, I was out night after night, eating, drinking and talking. I do not see any alternative. The public expect you to put in an appearance, especially at a time of year when they are all looking forward to the new season. You cannot divorce yourself from a project that is being run on your behalf.

So, despite my worthy intentions, I soon began to experience the problems of other beneficiaries. It was a much, much harder struggle than I had anticipated to lead such a double life, playing cricket by day and talking about it by night, and whenever I walked to the wicket I found it difficult to clear my mind and concentrate.

Even so, it was still a summer to stir the adrenalin of even the most lethargic cricketer, with the first Prudential World Cup, another series against Australia for the Ashes and at county level the prospect of playing under David Brown's leadership for Warwickshire.

Unfortunately, we could not maintain our good start to the season and finished up empty-handed. Injuries to Bill Bourne, Stephen Rouse and Bob Willis did not help, nor did the loss of five players – Jameson, Kanhai, Kallicharran, Murray and myself – during the fortnight of the Prudential Cup, and

Warwickshire simply did not pick up the threads afterwards.

Meanwhile, England were bitterly disappointed at losing to Australia in the semi-finals of the Prudential Cup at Headingley. Nor were we too impressed about the conditions for that match, which were poor indeed for one-day cricket, particularly a game of such importance.

It is now history that Gary Gilmour bowled us out rather rapidly and I am taking nothing away from his fine performance in telling this story, but we did think it rather unusual to find the pitch covered when we practised at Headingley the day before the match. The weather was overcast, but it was not raining.

When we peered underneath the covers we could see enough and when we commented on its greenness George Cawthray, the groundsman, said he had not had the weather to prepare the pitch he would have liked.

When we asked if he planned to take some of the grass off he said the could not remove any more. So, even before a ball was bowled, we could sense that this was hardly likely to be a good one-day pitch, especially at Leeds where the ball was likely to swing a great deal anyway.

So we expected problems when Ian Chappell put us in, but not perhaps from Gilmour. In Australia the previous winter I noticed that he had bowled the left-hander's normal inswinger for only a couple of overs; the ball had then stopped swinging and he had merely angled it across the right-hand batsman.

The surprising aspect of his bowling that morning at Leeds was not that Gilmour was again swinging the ball in, but on that green pitch the seam was biting and it was moving the other way after it pitched – an almost unplayable delivery. Another complication was that some balls were doing it, others were not.

One or two of our batsmen were dismissed playing back when they should have been forward, but I doubt if anyone not actually playing in that game appreciated just how much the ball was moving. Even when I watched television replays later I could not be sure that Gilmour was also cutting the ball away off the seam, but I knew from my own experience that he had.

Even then we might have won if we had held a couple of

catches, but the point would still have been made: this was a poor pitch for a one-day match. We learned later it had been used before (for an earlier Prudential match between Australia and Pakistan) and it seemed a pity – as well as a mystery – that a fresh pitch could not have been prepared for a game of such importance.

Much as we wanted to win the Prudential Cup, the series against Australia was almost always going to be the high point of the season for England. Now I had time to look ahead and reflect upon the psychological advantage that I knew Dennis Lillee had built up over me in Australia.

I tried to face up to this, although no other bowler had ever bothered me as much in my entire career, and I attempted to look at the series calmly and analytically. It seemed to me that the only way my confidence and that of other England batsmen could be restored was by facing Lillee and Jeff Thomson on good pitches, grinding them down and eventually proving to ourselves that we could make runs against them.

As the first Test was at Edgbaston, it could be in our favour because this is traditionally a pitch which is not noted for extravagant bounce and it usually becomes slower. After everything we had suffered in Australia the one thing we did not want was to be exposed to Thomson and Lillee on a rain-affected pitch.

So much for the dreams and theories of the out-of-form batsman! Mike Denness won the toss, put Australia in and we *were* caught on a rain-affected pitch, losing by an innings and eighty-five runs. It was a decision which was to cost Denness the England captaincy and one, had it been reversed, which could have changed the entire series.

The night before the Test, at our usual team meeting, Mike asked me, as the one player with local knowledge, how I thought the pitch would play. I put forward my theory about getting in on a 'flat' wicket and said the ball might seam around a little but would not bounce much.

When he asked me if I would consider putting Australia in, I said I thought we should bat, especially as the forecast was for unsettled weather. The next day I repeated this when he approached me again. Even if it meant struggling to make 250 or so against Thomson and Lillee and Walker under overcast conditions, we would still have the best of the pitch if the forecast was correct and therefore we must bat.

In fact, though the ball did not move around a great deal, we might well have bowled Australia out for around 250 but for dropping a few catches. That would have vindicated Denness's decision, but it would not have spared us from the Australian fast bowlers on a rain-affected pitch.

Long before the match was over the England team had lost heart because we were caught by Thomson and Lillee in conditions we could have avoided. I failed twice and in the second innings committed the error of taking my eye off the ball for a fraction of a second when Lillee bowled me a bouncer.

I was prepared to take it in the ribs or on the fleshy, upper part of my arm, but it struck my elbow and I temporarily retired hurt. The entire episode was probably a result of my problems in countering Lillee, but during that Test match I felt so weary that I admit my mental approach was not right.

After five successive series and three consecutive tours I thought it was time to examine my attitude to Test cricket. I wanted to play on regardless of failure, but questioned my ability to continue giving 100 per cent application to the job. I told no one about these self-doubts except my wife Jill and decided that rather than ask to be left out of the England team I would try to battle on.

This is the only realistic attitude a batsman can take when he strikes a lean spell. You keep going in bad patches, hoping that by some chance you will have a piece of luck here and there, that everything will gradually come right and that you will make a big score and thus regain your confidence and appetite for the game.

At the same time it takes a certain kind of moral courage for a man to stand up and admit that he is not mentally and physically equipped to play for his country at Test cricket. Looking back, I can see that I was not brave enough to ask to be omitted from the England team. Conscience does indeed make cowards of us all.

There is no doubt in my mind now that I should have asked to be left out. I could sense that I was slowing down. My legs felt like lead weights. I could not think clearly and I was so weary that I even rejected the regular game of squash which I have found helps to sharpen the reflexes.

H

The curious aspect of about my all-too-frequent failures against Lillee was that in the past I had always done well against bowlers I respected. He was the one exception to this, and the reason, I suppose, was that he had got right on top and I was so down, mentally, that he sensed he could get me out almost before he bowled a ball at me.

Off the field we remained extremely friendly. He did a lot to help one of my benefit functions go well. When we socialized we used to joke to each other about the way things had gone and I remember once saying I planned to have my revenge one day. He just laughed at that!

Meanwhile, the England captaincy changed hands again. Mike Denness had been faced with many real problems on his last two tours. Most of the time we had been struggling and he had been without two leading players in Geoff Boycott and John Snow in Australia.

Ironically, if we had batted first at Edgbaston, England might well have won and his position would have been strengthened, but now there was no doubt we needed a change. The team had hit rock bottom and desperately needed someone to come along and pick us up, to inspire us, to rebuild the team spirit of old.

In the eyes of many of us Tony Greig filled the bill. He was a dedicated, highly competitive player with a lot of personality. Equally importantly, his place in the team was beyond dispute because he had matured into a valuable all-rounder and he had the respect of everyone else in the side.

Soon after he was appointed he telephoned me, asking how I felt about moving down the order to number four. This came as no surprise because a selector had already broached the subject with me, while in Australia I knew that Greig had a theory that a spell away from the new ball would be good for me.

I agreed, so Barry Wood returned to open the innings, but the selection that surprised many people – including, I think it is fair to say, most of us in the England team – was that of David Steele, of Northamptonshire, who thus at the age of thirty-three was called up for his first Test match against the fire of Thomson and Lillee.

I regard Steele as a typical example of the hard-working county cricketer, maturing late in his career. He does not come from a particularly privileged background and has had to work hard for everything he has achieved in life. His guts and determination probably appealed to Greig as much as his ability.

His marvellous first series for England is now in the record books, but when he turned up at Lord's, this unassuming man with white hair and spectacles, I could not imagine anyone who looked less like an England batsman, let alone one who had been picked to combat Thomson and Lillee.

David's rather tatty kit helped to foster that impression and was the source of much mirth in the dressing-room. His gloves were ancient, torn and tattered, his boots looked as though they would fall apart at any moment and his flannels were so old that they actually did come adrift while he was batting in a later Test.

They all contrasted with his brand-new England sweater and cap which he wore with obvious pride. Before the game started I offered to give David a pair of old and infinitely grubby sweat bands to use while we practised. He accepted and, I learned later, used them in the middle for the rest of the series!

When he walked out for his first innings in a Test match he went down one flight of stairs too many in the Lord's pavilion and, instead of finding himself surrounded by Australians, found himself in the gentleman's toilet. But when he reached the middle he was not at all overawed and he played an innings which was a great psychological boost for everyone after our experiences in Australia and at Edgbaston.

Yet that morning, in the nets, Steele had been bowled so many times that he had stopped batting, his confidence apparently shaken. He walked across to me and said with a worried frown: 'How am I going to play? I haven't made a run for a week.'

I was hardly the ideal person to ask, but I tried to help. 'Just go out there and try to play the way you normally do,' I advised. 'After all, you have been selected for your ability and you are here on merit.'

Happily, Steele did just that. But there was nothing I could say to myself to change my depressing sequence of low scores against Australia. I failed again, falling twice more to Lillee, and as I walked back for the second time I knew there was no way the selectors could maintain their faith in me.

I blame only myself for not becoming re-established in the second innings. The situation was perfect. It was a beautiful pitch, we had runs on the board and were on top against Australia for once. And the solid, reassuring figure of John Edrich had compiled a century at the other end.

But the thought that I just *had* to make runs this time led me to play a poor stroke at a widish ball and that was that. Though I expected it, I was still disappointed when I found myself out of the team for the next Test and there was disappointment, too, when I rejoined Warwickshire.

We fell away in the John Player League, lost to Middlesex in the semi-finals of the Benson and Hedges Cup and for the rest of the season I hardly played a fluent innings. My footwork was sluggish and I seriously began to wonder if I was going into decline and if I had lost forever the ability to make runs at Test level.

I am still awaiting the answer to that question, of course. It may be that throughout my career I have tended to dwell introspectively on my failures when more outgoing players would have shrugged them off with a laugh and remembered the good times.

But if I am a perfectionist, never totally satisfied with my performances and always looking for ways to improve, I do not regard that as a fault. And if my story has seemed one of uncertainty, of triumph and disaster intermingled, well, cricket and life are like that.

Appendix I

Career Record – Test Cricket 1966–75

ENGLAND V WEST INDIES, 1966
The Oval, August 18. England won by an innings and 34 runs.
Amiss 17

ENGLAND V INDIA, 1967
Lord's, June 22. England won by an innings and 124 runs.
Amiss 29
Edgbaston, July 13. England won by 132 runs.
Amiss 5 and 45

ENGLAND V PAKISTAN, 1967
The Oval, August 24. England won by eight wickets.
Amiss 26 and 3 not out

ENGLAND V AUSTRALIA, 1968
Old Trafford, June 6. Australia won by 159 runs.
Amiss 0 and 0

ENGLAND V REST OF THE WORLD, 1970
The Oval, August 13. Rest of World won by four wickets.
Amiss 24 and 35

ENGLAND V PAKISTAN, 1971
Edgbaston, June 3. Drawn.
Amiss 4 and 22
Lord's, June 17. Drawn.
Amiss 19 not out
Headingley, July 8. England won by 25 runs.
Amiss 23 and 56

ENGLAND V INDIA, 1971
Lord's, July 22. Drawn.
Amiss 9 and 0

MCC V INDIA, 1972/3

New Delhi, December 20. England won by six wickets.
Amiss 46 and 9
Calcutta, December 30. India won by 28 runs.
Amiss 11 and 1
Madras, January 12. India won by four wickets.
Amiss 15 and 8

MCC V PAKISTAN, 1973

Lahore, March 2. Drawn.
Amiss 112 and 16
Hyderabad, March 16. Drawn.
Amiss 158 and 0
Karachi, March 24. Drawn.
Amiss 99 and 21 not out

ENGLAND V NEW ZEALAND, 1973

Trent Bridge, June 7. England won by 38 runs.
Amiss 42 and 138 not out
Lord's, June 21. Drawn.
Amiss 9 and 53
Headingley, July 5. England won by an innings and one run.
Amiss 8

ENGLAND V WEST INDIES, 1973

The Oval, July 26. West Indies won by 158 runs.
Amiss 29 and 15
Edgbaston, August 9. Drawn.
Amiss 56 and 86 not out
Lord's, August 23. West Indies won by an innings and 226 runs.
Amiss 35 and 10

MCC V WEST INDIES, 1974

Port of Spain, February 2. West Indies won by 7 wickets.
Amiss 6 and 174
Kingston, February 16. Drawn.
Amiss 27 and 262 not out
Bridgetown, March 6. Drawn.
Amiss 12 and 4
Georgetown, March 22. Drawn.
Amiss 118
Port of Spain, March 30. England won by 26 runs.
Amiss 44 and 16

Appendix I 111

ENGLAND V INDIA, 1974
Old Trafford, June 6. England won by 113 runs.
Amiss 56 and 47
Lord's, June 20. England won by an innings and 285 runs.
Amiss 188
Edgbaston, July 4. England won by an innings and 78 runs
Amiss 79

ENGLAND V PAKISTAN, 1974
Headingley, July 25. Drawn.
Amiss 13 and 8
Lord's, August 8. Drawn.
Amiss 2 and 14 not out
The Oval, August 22. Drawn.
Amiss 183

MCC V AUSTRALIA, 1974/5
Brisbane, November 29. Australia won by 166 runs.
Amiss 7 and 25
Melbourne, December 26. Drawn.
Amiss 4 and 90
Sydney, January 4. Australia won by 171 runs.
Amiss 12 and 37
Adelaide, January 26. Australia won by 163 runs.
Amiss 0 and 0
Melbourne, February 8. England won by an innings and 4 runs.
Amiss 0

MCC V NEW ZEALAND, 1975
Auckland, February 20. England won by an innings and 83 runs.
Amiss 19
Christchurch, March 2. Drawn.
Amiss 164 not out

ENGLAND V AUSTRALIA, 1975
Edgbaston, July 10. Australia won by an innings and 85 runs.
Amiss 4 and 5
Lord's, July 31. Drawn.
Amiss 0 and 10

Appendix II

Career Record – Test Match Summary

Season	Opponents	Matches	Innings	Not Out	Highest Score	Runs	Average	100s	Catches
1966	West Indies	1	1	—	17	17	17·00	—	—
1967	India	2	3	—	45	79	26·33	—	4
1967	Pakistan	1	2	1	26	29	29·00	—	—
1968	Australia	1	2	—	0	0	0·00	—	—
1970	Rest of World	1	2	—	35	59	29·50	—	1
1971	Pakistan	3	5	1	56	124	31·00	—	1
1971	India	1	2	—	9	9	4·50	—	2
1972–73	India	3	6	—	46	90	15·00	—	1
1972–73	Pakistan	3	6	1	158	406	81·20	2	2
1973	New Zealand	3	5	1	138*	250	62·50	1	—
1973	West Indies	3	6	1	86*	231	46·20	—	2
1973–74	West Indies	5	9	1	262*	663	82·87	3	—
1974	India	3	4	—	188	370	92·50	3	—
1974	Pakistan	3	5	1	183	220	55·00	1	1

1974–75 Australia	5	9	—	90	175	19·44	—	3
1974–75 New Zealand	2	2	1	164*	183	91·50	1	3
1975 Australia	2	4	—	10	19	4·75	—	1

v Australia	8	15	—	90	194	12·93	—	4
v West Indies	9	16	2	262*	911	65·07	3	2
v New Zealand	5	7	2	164*	433	86·60	2	3
v India	9	15	—	188	548	36·53	1	7
v Pakistan	10	18	4	183	779	55·64	3	4
v Rest of World	1	2	—	35	59	29·50	—	1

Debut: 1966 v West Indies, 5th Test (The Oval)
Highest Score: 262 not out v West Indies (Kingston) 1973–74

Appendix III

Batting Career Record – All First-Class Matches

	Season	Matches	Innings	Not Out	Highest Score	Runs	Average	100s	Catches
Warwickshire	1960	7	9	3	43*	135	22·50	—	2
Warwickshire	1961	4	7	—	41	106	15·14	—	1
Warwickshire	1962	9	15	1	62	352	25·14	—	7
Warwickshire	1963	9	17	1	58	312	19·50	—	6
Warwickshire	1964	8	16	3	114	307	23·61	1	6
Warwickshire	1965	32	53	2	86	1433	28·09	—	23
Warwickshire	1966	29	52	5	160*	1765	37·55	2	14
MCC Under-25 in Pakistan	1966–67	7	11	2	131	575	63·88	2	5
Warwickshire	1967	26	43	9	176*	1850	54·41	5	25
International XI in Pakistan, India & Ceylon	1967–68	4	8	1	109	271	38·71	1	8
Warwickshire	1968	30	46	4	128	1222	29·09	2	24
Warwickshire	1969	30	51	3	120	1539	32·06	1	24
Warwickshire	1970	27	48	10	110	1757	46·23	2	26

	Season				HS	Runs	Avge		
Rest of World XI in Pakistan	1970–71	1	2	—	34	36	18·00	—	—
Warwickshire	1971	25	37	3	124	1294	38·05	2	13
Warwickshire	1972	18	29	7	192	1219	55·40	5	14
MCC in India, Ceylon & Pakistan	1972–73	12	23	4	158	861	45·31	2	5
Warwickshire	1973	23	39	9	146*	1634	54·46	3	13
MCC in West Indies	1973–74	9	16	1	262*	1120	74·66	5	3
Warwickshire	1974	18	31	3	195	1510	53·92	5	6
MCC in Australia & New Zealand	1974–75	15	23	2	164*	982	46·76	3	12
Warwickshire	1975	16	32	2	158*	1422	47·40	3	21

Debut: 1960 Warwickshire v Surrey (The Oval) – aged 17
Highest Score: 262* England v West Indies (Kingston) 1973–74
Highest Score (UK): 195 Warwickshire v Middlesex (Edgbaston) 1974

Bowling (1960–1975)

Overs	Matches	Runs	Wickets	Average
165.2	25	603	15	40·20

Best bowling: 3 for 21 Warwickshire v Middlesex (Lord's) 1970

Index

Compiled by J. F. Baker